Learning iOS UI Development

Implement complex iOS user interfaces with ease using Swift

Yari D'areglia

[PACKT] open source*
community experience distilled

PUBLISHING

BIRMINGHAM - MUMBAI

Learning iOS UI Development

First published: December 2015

Production reference: 1181215

Published by Packt Publishing Ltd.
Livery Place
35 Livery Street
Birmingham B3 2PB, UK.

ISBN 978-1-78528-819-7

www.packtpub.com

Credits

Author
Yari D'areglia

Reviewers
Nicola Armellini
Christian Stehno

Commissioning Editor
Nadeem N. Bagban

Acquisition Editor
Manish Nainani

Content Development Editor
Rashmi Suvarna

Technical Editor
Humera Shaikh

Copy Editor
Shruti Iyer

Project Coordinator
Judie Jose

Proofreader
Safis Editing

Indexer
Monica Ajmera Mehta

Graphics
Jason Monteiro

Production Coordinator
Nilesh Mohite

Cover Work
Nilesh Mohite

About the Author

Yari D'areglia is a developer with 15 years of experience in software architecture and development. During the last 4 years, he built successful iOS and OS X applications for developers as well as the mainstream public.

Yari, together with Nicola Armellini, founded Jumpzero, a company based in Italy that released countless mobile, desktop, and web applications.

Currently, he is employed as a senior iOS engineer at Neato Robotics, a company based in Silicon Valley, where he works on the communication between robots and iOS devices.

Yari writes at `www.ThinkAndBuild.it`, a blog focused on iOS development with a strong focus on user interface development.

You can reach him on Twitter at `@bitwaker`.

I'd like to thank Nicola Armellini for taking the time to review this book and teaching me countless things about my work and life. Thanks, brother!

Special thanks go to my future wife, Lorena. She was extremely supportive and accepted all my "I'm busy, honey; I need to finish this chapter..." with a gentle smile. You are awesome; I love you.

Thanks, mom, your ragù and your words were both of vital importance during the writing of the last few chapters. You're a strong woman, and I'm proud to be your son.

Many thanks and appreciation go to everyone who contributed to the production of this book: Manish, Ritika, Rashmi, and Humera. Thank you for being so kind and professional.

Last but not least, I would like to thank my greatest friends, Simo, Luke, and Stefano (Panzer). Our next role-playing session is on its way.

About the Reviewers

Nicola Armellini is a designer from Italy who constantly crosses the boundary between technology and communication.

First approaching the industry through the video game medium, he partnered with Yari D'Areglia and founded Jumpzero, specializing in the user experience and interface design of OS X and iOS applications. At the same time, Nicola helped grow the audience of Yari's *Think & Build* blog by editing and reviewing his in-depth tutorial articles.

A fan of redistributing knowledge and making it accessible, he taught his craft and its implications in terms of marketing and communication as a lecturer at European Institute of Design in Milan.

As a side project slowly turned into his main focus, Nicola started fiddling with virtual reality and exploring new ways of interacting with machines and CG environments, questioning the status quo of how information is presented and manipulated.

He now studies to become an aerospace engineer and can be found at
nicolaarmellini.com.

Christian Stehno studied computer science and got his diploma from the University of Oldenburg in 2000. Since then, he has worked on different topics in computer science. As researcher on theoretical computer science at University, Christian switched to embedded system design at a research institute later on. In 2010, he started his own company, CoSynth, which develops embedded systems and intelligent cameras for industrial automation. In addition, Christian is a long-time member of the Irrlicht 3D Engine developer team.

www.PacktPub.com

Support files, eBooks, discount offers, and more

For support files and downloads related to your book, please visit www.PacktPub.com.

Did you know that Packt offers eBook versions of every book published, with PDF and ePub files available? You can upgrade to the eBook version at www.PacktPub.com and as a print book customer, you are entitled to a discount on the eBook copy. Get in touch with us at service@packtpub.com for more details.

At www.PacktPub.com, you can also read a collection of free technical articles, sign up for a range of free newsletters and receive exclusive discounts and offers on Packt books and eBooks.

https://www2.packtpub.com/books/subscription/packtlib

Do you need instant solutions to your IT questions? PacktLib is Packt's online digital book library. Here, you can search, access, and read Packt's entire library of books.

Why subscribe?

- Fully searchable across every book published by Packt
- Copy and paste, print, and bookmark content
- On demand and accessible via a web browser

Free access for Packt account holders

If you have an account with Packt at www.PacktPub.com, you can use this to access PacktLib today and view 9 entirely free books. Simply use your login credentials for immediate access.

To my father, Max.

Table of Contents

Preface

Through this comprehensive one-stop guide, you'll get to grips with the entire UIKit framework and creating modern user interfaces for your iOS devices using Swift. Starting with an overview of the iOS drawing system and available tools, you will learn how to use these technologies to create adaptable layouts and custom elements for your applications. You'll then be introduced to other topics such as animation and code drawing with core graphics, which will give you all the knowledge you need to create astonishing user interfaces. By the time you reach the end of this book, you will have a solid foundation in iOS user interface development and have gained a valuable insight into the process of building firm and complex UIs.

What this book covers

Chapter 1, UI Fundamentals, starts by describing how interfaces are structured and drawn and then presents some really important elements, such as windows and views.

Chapter 2, UI Components Overview – UIKit, is an overview of the UIKit framework. It's a guided tour through the main UIKit elements, from their usage inside an app to their customization.

Chapter 3, Interface Builder, XIB, and Storyboard, gives an overview of the Xcode tools used to set up and build UIs.

Chapter 4, Auto Layout, is the key to understanding how Auto Layout works. It describes in detail how to create dynamic layouts.

Chapter 5, Adaptive User Interfaces, discusses a very important topic: how to improve user experience and provide interfaces that can adapt to different orientations, screen sizes, and user preferences using the latest advancements introduced with iOS 8 and 9.

Chapter 6, Layers and Core Animation, focuses on CALayer in the context of core animation. It illustrates how to achieve animations in iOS using two different approaches.

Chapter 7, UI Interactions – Touches and Gestures, analyzes the main way users interact with UIs—through touch. It answers questions such as "how is this information passed from the screen to the views?" and "how can we build an engaging UI using gestures?"

Chapter 8, How to Build Custom Controls, explains how to build custom controls after learning how these controls work in the previous chapters.

Chapter 9, Introduction to Core Graphics, is a final quick overview of the core graphics (Quartz 2D) framework to show you how to perform custom drawings with iOS.

What you need for this book

In order to be able to run the code examples, you need a Mac computer with OS X and Xcode installed. The suggested minimal version is OS X 10.11.1 and Xcode 7.1.

Who this book is for

This easy-to-follow guide is perfect for beginner-level iOS developers who want to become proficient in user interface development. It is also useful for experienced iOS developers who need a complete overview of this broad topic all in one place without having to consult various sources.

Conventions

In this book, you will find a number of text styles that distinguish between different kinds of information. Here are some examples of these styles and an explanation of their meaning.

Code words in text, database table names, folder names, filenames, file extensions, pathnames, dummy URLs, user input, and Twitter handles are shown as follows: "The properties that define the view geometry are `frame`, `bounds`, and `center` and they are configured using the geometry structures you just saw."

A block of code is set as follows:

```
// Define a point
let point = CGPoint(x: 20, y: 10)

// Define a size
let size = CGSize(width: 20, height: 10)

// Define a rect using size and point
let rect_A = CGRect(origin: point, size: size)

// Define a rect using x, y, width and height data
let rect_B = CGRect(x: 15, y: 10, width: 100, height: 30)
```

When we wish to draw your attention to a particular part of a code block, the relevant lines or items are set in bold:

```
enum UIUserInterfaceSizeClass : Int {
    case Unspecified
    case Compact
    case Regular
}
```

New terms and **important words** are shown in bold. Words that you see on the screen, for example, in menus or dialog boxes, appear in the text like this: "Create a new asset by clicking on the **+** symbol and selecting **New Image Asset**."

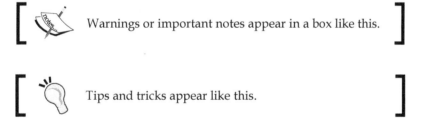

Warnings or important notes appear in a box like this.

Tips and tricks appear like this.

Reader feedback

Feedback from our readers is always welcome. Let us know what you think about this book—what you liked or disliked. Reader feedback is important for us as it helps us develop titles that you will really get the most out of.

To send us general feedback, simply e-mail feedback@packtpub.com, and mention the book's title in the subject of your message.

If there is a topic that you have expertise in and you are interested in either writing or contributing to a book, see our author guide at www.packtpub.com/authors.

Customer support

Now that you are the proud owner of a Packt book, we have a number of things to help you to get the most from your purchase.

Downloading the example code

You can download the example code files from your account at http://www.packtpub.com for all the Packt Publishing books you have purchased. If you purchased this book elsewhere, you can visit http://www.packtpub.com/support and register to have the files e-mailed directly to you.

Downloading the color images of this book

We also provide you with a PDF file that has color images of the screenshots/diagrams used in this book. The color images will help you better understand the changes in the output. You can download this file from https://www.packtpub.com/sites/default/files/downloads/LearningiOSUIDevelopment_Graphics.pdf.

Errata

Although we have taken every care to ensure the accuracy of our content, mistakes do happen. If you find a mistake in one of our books—maybe a mistake in the text or the code—we would be grateful if you could report this to us. By doing so, you can save other readers from frustration and help us improve subsequent versions of this book. If you find any errata, please report them by visiting http://www.packtpub.com/submit-errata, selecting your book, clicking on the **Errata Submission Form** link, and entering the details of your errata. Once your errata are verified, your submission will be accepted and the errata will be uploaded to our website or added to any list of existing errata under the Errata section of that title.

To view the previously submitted errata, go to https://www.packtpub.com/books/content/support and enter the name of the book in the search field. The required information will appear under the **Errata** section.

Piracy

Piracy of copyrighted material on the Internet is an ongoing problem across all media. At Packt, we take the protection of our copyright and licenses very seriously. If you come across any illegal copies of our works in any form on the Internet, please provide us with the location address or website name immediately so that we can pursue a remedy.

Please contact us at copyright@packtpub.com with a link to the suspected pirated material.

We appreciate your help in protecting our authors and our ability to bring you valuable content.

Questions

If you have a problem with any aspect of this book, you can contact us at questions@packtpub.com, and we will do our best to address the problem.

1
UI Fundamentals

Creating a successful application is not only a matter of writing efficient and reliable code. User interfaces and experience are relevant topics that we have to seriously take into account during the development process. If you want to be able to create appealing and well-structured layouts, you need to become familiar with the main building blocks of user interfaces.

In this chapter, we will explore the basics of iOS UI development, which you will use and improve upon for the rest of the book and, hopefully, for the rest of your career.

We will start from the fundamental actors of a user interface, such as windows and views; then, we will connect the dots showing how all these components work together by creating a UI hierarchy and how the system interacts with all these elements.

Let's start our journey from the element at the top of the stack: the window.

Exploring windows

A window is an instance of the UIWindow class, and it is the topmost element of any application UI's hierarchy. It doesn't draw any visual object and can be considered as a blank container for the UI elements called **views**. An application must have at least one window that normally fills the entire screen.

One of the main roles of the window is to *deliver touches* to the underlying views. You'll read more about this topic in *Chapter 7, UI Interactions – Touches and Gestures*. For now, it suffices to say that a window is the first entry point for a touch event. The touch is then pushed down through the view hierarchy until it reaches the right view.

The contents of windows

The contents of your applications are mainly directed by *view controllers* and presented through views, which, in turn, are displayed inside a window. As you will learn in the next section, this sequence is automatically handled by iOS, and all the classes involved in the process are organized to interact seamlessly.

The easiest and most reliable way to send content to a window is by configuring its `rootViewController` property with a `UIViewController` instance. The view controller's view will automatically be set as the contents of the window and presented to the user.

This solution simplifies the window hierarchy, ensuring that contents are all children of the same root. Thanks to this solution, changing the contents of a window is just a matter of updating its root view controller.

While you'll learn more about view controllers and views in the next paragraphs, this image should clarify how all these objects cooperate to present their contents to the user:

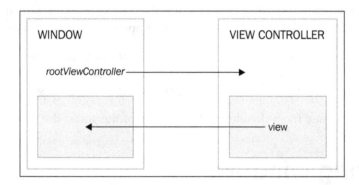

The view controller is initialized and set as the root view controller of the window. Finally, the window presents the current root view controller's view.

Configuring windows

You rarely need to set up a window manually. In most cases, Xcode defines all the needed information for you. Let's take a look at the entire process to better understand what goes on under the hood.

When you create a new Xcode project using the wizard, a Storyboard is created for you. If you check the `info.plist` file, you'll see that the `Main storyboard filebase name` key reports the name of the Storyboard by default as `Main`:

Application requires iPhone...		Boolean	YES
Launch screen interface file base...		String	LaunchScreen
Main storyboard file base name		String	Main
▶ Required device capabilities		Array	(1 item)
Status bar style		String	UIStatusBarStyleLightContent

This key is really important as it tells Xcode that you want to start the application from the Storyboard or, more precisely, from the *Storyboard initial view controller* (the one indicated by the grey arrow inside the Storyboard working area).

The `@UIApplicationMain` attribute in the `AppDelegate.swift` file is responsible for the launch of the entire application process. It marks an entry point for the application launch, reading the Storyboard's information from the `info.plist` file and instantiating the *initial view controller*.

At this point, a `UIWindow` instance is created and associated with the `window` property of the `AppDelegate` class. This property will be a handy reference to the main window for the entire life cycle of the application.

The initial view controller, previously initialized, is now assigned to the `rootViewController` property of the window; therefore, the initial view controller's *view* becomes the current window's content.

Since windows are invisible by default, there is one last step required to show the content to the user. After the `application:didFinishLaunchingWithOptions` function finishes its execution, `makeKeyAndVisible` is called for the window, which now loads its interface from `rootViewController` and finally displays it contents.

The following image summarizes all these steps:

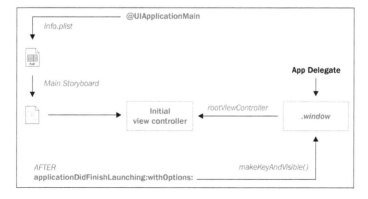

The same result can be obtained programmatically. If you remove the `Main storyboard filebase name` key from the `info.plist` file, Xcode doesn't have any information on how to set up a valid window. The `application:didiFinishLau nchingWithOptions` function is the right place to manually instantiate it. You can execute the following:

```
func application(application: UIApplication,
    didFinishLaunchingWithOptions
    launchOptions: [NSObject: AnyObject]?) -> Bool {

    // Instantiate a window with the same size of the screen
    window = UIWindow(frame: UIScreen.mainScreen().bounds)
    // Instantiate a view controller with the Main storyboard
    let storyboard = UIStoryboard(name: "Main", bundle: nil)
    let viewController = storyboard.instantiateViewController
        WithIdentifier("viewController2") as! ViewController

    // Setup and present the window
    window?.rootViewController = viewController
    window?.makeKeyAndVisible()

    return true
}
```

As you can note, this code retraces the same steps that we saw previously. The only noteworthy thing is the way the window frame is defined: `UIScreen` is a class that represents a screen device. In the previous block of code, the `mainScreen` function is used to get the current device bounds and build a window that is the same size as the screen.

Downloading the example code

You can download the example code files for all Packt books you have purchased from your account at http://www.packtpub.com. If you purchased this book elsewhere, you can visit http://www.packtpub.com/support and register to have the files e-mailed directly to you.

Working with views

Along your path of UI enlightenment, you'll encounter different types of views. You can simplify the categorization by thinking about a view as the atomic element of the user interface, where a view has its own specific properties and can be grouped with other views to create complex hierarchies.

`UIView` is the base class used to instantiate generic views and it can be subclassed to create custom views. Almost all the UI elements that you will use in your applications are inherited from this class, and in the next chapter, you'll learn a lot about some of the elements provided by Apple within the **UIKit** framework.

> Keep in mind that the `UIWindow` class too is a subclass of `UIView`. This is generally a cause of confusion considering that in a UI hierarchy, views are the children of a window and not the other way around.

A `UIView` instance has properties that you can use to change an aspect of the view. For example, the `backgroundColor` property accepts `UIColor` to define a tint for the view's background. The background of a view is transparent by default, and as you'll see later in this chapter, some views can seep through other views.

The `alpha` property is useful if your view and all the elements it contains need to be transparent. It accepts a value from `0.0` to `1.0`, and depending on your settings, it gives the view a "see-through" effect. With the help of this property, you can hide or unhide a view using some interesting animations, as you will learn in *Chapter 6, Layers and Core Animation*.

Another way to change the visibility of a view is using the `hidden` property, which can be set to `true` or `false`.

It's important to note that when you hide a view using the `hidden` or `alpha` properties, you are not removing the view from the hierarchy and memory; the view can, in fact, still be reached, but the interaction with the user is automatically disabled until the view is visible again. This is a neat trick to temporarily remove a view from the screen, thus preventing any unintended interaction.

Sometimes, you might need to disable a view even if the drawing goes on (for example, you may want to be sure that the UI interactions are disabled while loading some external data). In this case, you may find the `userInteractionEnabled` property useful; setting this property to `false` tells the view to ignore user events.

Defining the view's geometry

The properties of some view's have only one role: defining how the view is drawn on screen. Before diving into a description of these properties, it's worth introducing the structures that are involved in the definition of the view geometry:

- CGPoint: This is defined by two properties, x and y, and it represents a single point

- CGSize: This is defined by two properties, width and height, and it represents a generic size

- CGRect: This is defined by two properties, origin (CGPoint) and size (CGSize), and it represents a quadrilateral area

 When working with iOS, you will encounter different coordinate systems. With UIViews, the origin of the coordinate system (x: 0, y: 0) is on the upper-left side. The x value increases from left to right, and the y value increases from top to bottom.

The code needed to initialize these structures is straightforward, and there are a lot of functionalities provided by Apple that simplify our work with these structures.

The following code shows how to create the Rect, Size, and Point instances:

```
// Define a point
let point = CGPoint(x: 20, y: 10)

// Define a size
let size = CGSize(width: 20, height: 10)

// Define a rect using size and point
let rect_A = CGRect(origin: point, size: size)

// Define a rect using x, y, width and height data
let rect_B = CGRect(x: 15, y: 10, width: 100, height: 30)
```

The properties that define the view geometry are frame, bounds, and center and they are configured using the geometry structures you just saw.

The bounds property

Let's start with the bounds property. It is a CGRect property that defines information (*size* and *origin*) locally to the view. This means that when we speak about bounds, we do not determine how the view is drawn in the UI hierarchy but how it's drawn in a decontextualized, local space. You'll read more about UI hierarchy later in this chapter; for now, just think about it as a structure that organizes trees of views, where a view can be either the child or parent of another view. That said, in most cases, the origin bound is (x:0, y:0), while the size property is the size of the view.

The frame property

On the other hand, the frame property defines how a view is placed inside the hierarchy. It's a CGRect property similar to bounds, but its origin value determines how the view is placed inside its *parent* view.

At this point, we might conclude that frame and bounds are similar; however, this is not always true. Take a look at the following images to better understand how they work together to define the view geometry:

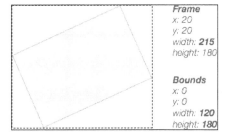

In this case, frame and bounds have the same size, but the position values are different. Take a look at this image:

This indicates that after a rotation, the same view maintains the bounds, while the frame changes significantly, adapting its size in order to contain the rotated view.

The center property

The center property works in relation to the UI hierarchy (as does the frame), and it's a handy way to define the view's position inside its parent. It differs from frame.origin in the way its position is calculated. With frame, the origin position is calculated using the upper-left corner of the view, while for the center, the anchor is the view's center, as you can see from the following image:

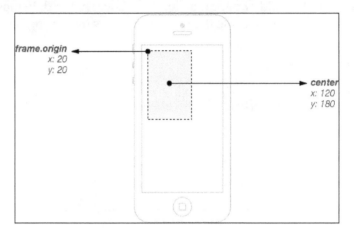

UI hierarchy and views inheritance

In this chapter, we already talked about UI hierarchies. Let's dive into the topic by introducing the concepts of *subview* and *superview* and learning how to build and manage complex hierarchies.

Every instance of UIView (or its subclass) can be connected with other views in a parent-child relationship. The parent view is called **superview**, while the children are called **subviews**. A view can only have one superview, but it can contain more than one subview:

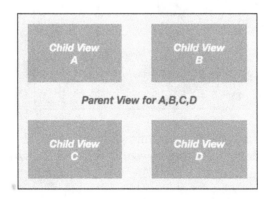

Thanks to the dedicated `UIView` properties and functions, you can easily inspect a view hierarchy and navigate from a root view down through to the last view of the hierarchy.

A view can access its parent from the `superview` property, as follows:

```
let parentView = view.superview
```

The property returns a single `UIView` reference or `nil` if the view is not added to the hierarchy yet.

In a similar way, the `subviews` property returns an array of `UIView` instances that are the children of the view. Take a look at this code:

```
let children = view.subviews
```

Managing with the hierarchy

The `UIView` class offers helpful functions to add, move, and delete elements from the hierarchy; you can call these functions directly from the view instances.

The `addSubview:` function pushes a view as the child of the caller, as follows:

```
containerView.addSubview(childView)
```

Views that are added as subviews of the same view are *sibling*. Sibling subviews are assigned to an *index* based on the order of insertion, which in turn corresponds to the drawing order — the highest index is drawn at the front, while the lowest is drawn behind the other sibling views. The `addSubview:` function assigns the first free index to the view, determining its position, which is in front of all the other views with lower indexes.

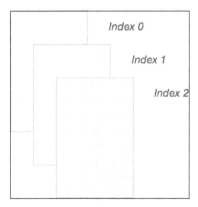

This order can be manipulated using functions that specify the desired index in an absolute or relative way:

```
containerView.insertSubview(childView, atIndex: 2)
```

With the `insertSubview:atIndex` function, you can specify an index in which to place the view. If the index is not free, the view at this index gets shifted up by one index, consequently shifting all the other sibling views with indexes greater than the requested one.

With the same logic, a view can be placed into the hierarchy using another view as a reference and specifying that the new view should be inserted above (`insertSubview:aboveSubview`) or below (`insertSubview:belowSubview`) the referenced view, as follows:

```
containerView.insertSubview(childView, aboveSubview: anotherView)

containerView.insertSubview(childView, belowSubview: anotherView)
```

Removing a view from the hierarchy is extremely simple. If you have a reference of the view that you want to remove, just call the `removeFromSuperview` function for this view. Alternatively, if you want to remove all the subviews from the parent view, just loop through the subviews and remove the views one by one. You can use the following code for this:

```
for subview in container.subviews {
    subview.removeFromSuperview()
}
```

When you remove a view from the hierarchy, you are removing its subviews as well. If you haven't defined any reference to the views, they are no longer retained in memory; therefore, all chances to get access to the views are lost.

When you need to access a subview on the fly without saving a reference to it, you can use the `tag` property. A `UIView` instance can be easily marked using an integer, and you can obtain the view that corresponds to the same tag using the `viewWithTag;` function. This function returns the view itself or the first subview whose tag coincides with the requested tag.

View and subview visibility

A parent view defines its subviews' visibility outside its boundaries through the Boolean property `clipToBounds`. If this property is `true`, the view behaves as a mask for its subviews, preventing them from being drawn outside the boundaries. The following image presents the result of different `clipToBounds` values on the same hierarchy:

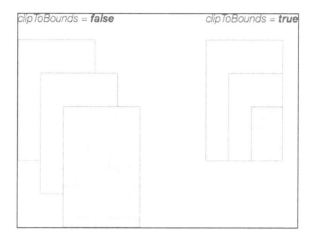

Another important note about subview visibility is related to the `alpha` property, which, as we mentioned previously, defines the opacity of the view. Subviews indirectly inherit the alpha value from their superviews, so the resulting opacity of the subview depends both on their parent and their own alpha.

If your view has a nontransparent background, it is good practice to leave the `opaque` property set to `true` as a hint for the drawing system. Opaque views are optimized for this. The opposite is suggested if the view is fully or partially transparent; set this property to `false`.

Hierarchy events

Changes on the hierarchy can be intercepted and managed through callbacks called on the parent and child views.

When a view is attached to a superview, the `didMoveToSuperview` function is called. If we want to perform a task after this event is triggered, we have to override this function with a `UIView` subclass by executing the following code:

```
class CustomView: UIView {

    override func didMoveToSuperview() {
        println("I have a superview!")
    }
}
```

In the same way, the event can be intercepted by the superview overriding the `didAddSubview:subview` function, as follows:

```
override func didAddSubview(subview: UIView) {
    println("The subview \(subview) has been added")
}
```

The view will be added to a hierarchy that has a window as root. At this point, the `didMoveToWindow` event is called. After the event is triggered, the `window` property of the view instance becomes a reference to the root window; this turns out to be a handy way to check whether a view has reached the screen.

Remember that the only way to show a view on screen is through a window; so, if the `window` property is `nil`, you can be sure that the view is not added to a window hierarchy yet and that, for this reason, it won't be visible. Take a look at this code:

```
override func didMoveToWindow() {
    println("I've been attached to this window hierarchy: \(window)")
}
```

Another important method that responds to hierarchy changes is `layoutSubviews`. This function is called as soon as a subview is added to or removed from the hierarchy and every time the bounds of the view change. Within this function, *Auto Layout constraints* (more on this will be discussed in *Chapter 5, Adaptive User Interfaces*) are read, and they act to organize the subview's layout. You can override this function to perform your customizations to the layout, adding or tweaking the current constraints.

Notes about debug

When views are complex, the hierarchy is hardly straightforward. Xcode helps you, though, with an interesting debug instrument. When your application is running, select Debug -> View Debugging -> Capture View Hierarchy from the Xcode menu, and you'll see an interactive 3D representation of the current view hierarchy showing the depth and the position of all the views contained:

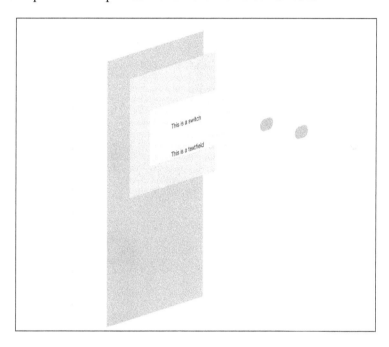

Hands-on code

In this section, you will practice some of the concepts that we just discussed by writing a real application.

Open the Chapter 1 folder and launch the . . .\Start\Chapter1 project. You'll find a simple application structure that is the starting point for this exercise; the final result is the . . .\Completed\Chapter1 project.

The base structure is really simple: an uppermost area with some controls (two buttons and one segmented control) and a view (with a light gray background) that we call a *container*:

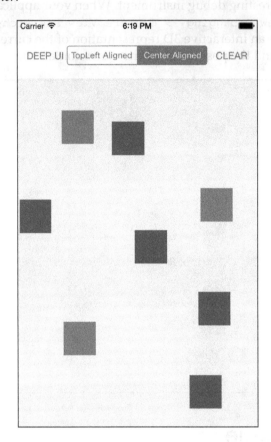

Your goal is to implement the `createView:` function that receives a location (`CGPoint`) and adds a subview at this location inside the container. Depending on the value of the segmented control, you should use the received location as the center (red views) or upper-left corner of the new view (blue views). You need to also implement the `clear` function to remove all the added subviews. The project implements a *tap gesture* on the container, which invokes `createView` linked to the touch location.

Let's implement the `createView` function for the `viewController.swift` file first by executing the following:

```
func createView(location:CGPoint){
    let viewSize = CGSize(width: 50, height: 50)
    let viewFrame = CGRect(origin: location, size: viewSize)
```

```
    let childView = UIView(frame: viewFrame)
    childView.backgroundColor = UIColor.redColor()
    viewContainer.addSubview(childView)

    if isCenterAligned {
        childView.center = location
        childView.backgroundColor = UIColor.blueColor()
    }
}
```

The `childView` function is instantiated using a fixed size and the received location as its origin. Then, it is simply attached to `viewContainer` using `addSubview`. If the `isCenterAligned` property (which is handled by the segmented control) is `true`, the `center` property of the view is moved to the received location.

The implementation of the `clear` function is straightforward, as you can note in the following code:

```
@IBAction func clear(){
for subview in viewContainer.subviews{
        subview.removeFromSuperview()
    }
}
```

It just performs a loop through the `viewContainer` subviews to call the `removeFromSuperview` function on these subviews.

A second functionality can be added to this exercise. Push the "Deep" button on the upper-left side of the screen, and debug the current hierarchy using the "capture view hierarchy" function to see this great feature in action!

View drawing and life cycle

iOS uses remarkable optimizations in the process of drawing contents on screen. Views are not continuously drawn; the system draws any view just once and creates snapshots for each displayed element. The current snapshot is shown until a view doesn't require an update. The view is then redrawn, and a new snapshot for the updated view is taken. This is a clever way to avoid a wastage of resources. In devices such as smartphones, optimization is mandatory.

The `UIView` content can be invalidated by calling the `setNeedsDisplay:` or `setNeedsDisplayInRect:` function.

This call basically tells the drawing system that the view content needs to be updated with a new version. Later, during the next run loop, the system asks the view to redraw. The main difference between the `setNeedsDisplay:` and `setNeedsDisplayInRect:` functions is that the latter performs an optimization using only a portion of the new view content.

In most cases, the redrawing process is managed for you by UIKit. If you need to create your really custom `UIView` subclass, though, you probably want to draw the contents of the view yourself. In this case, the `drawRect:` function is the place where you will add the drawing functions. You'll learn more about custom drawing in *Chapters 6, Layers and Core Animation*, and *Chapter 9, Introduction to Core Graphics*. For now, it suffices to say that you should never call this function directly! When the content of the view needs to be updated, just call `setNeedDisplay:` and the `drawRect:` function will be executed by the system following the right procedure.

Here is a quick example of custom drawing with which we can create a `UIView` subclass that draws a simple red ellipse at the center of the view:

```
import UIKit

class ellipseView: UIView {

    override func drawRect(rect: CGRect) {

        let path = UIBezierPath(ovalInRect: self.bounds)
        UIColor.redColor().setStroke()
        UIColor.orangeColor().setFill()
        path.fill()
        path.stroke()

    }
}
```

This function uses `UIBezierPath` to define an oval shape that has a stroke and fill of red and orange. This shape is finally drawn in the current *Graphic Context*, which can be seen as an empty dashboard where you can design using code. You'll learn more about Graphic Contexts in *Chapter 9, Introduction to Core Graphics*.

View controllers and views

The `UIViewController` property `view` is the root view of the hierarchy that defines the view controller's contents. As we already saw, a view controller is associated with the window's `rootViewController` property, and a connection is established between the `window` property of the view controller `view` and the window.

During its life cycle, a view controller deals with important events related to its view. Depending on your needs, you might find these events useful for the UI definition.

Here is a quick but complete description of the functions called in relation to these events:

Function	Description
loadView	This is called when the view is created and assigned to the view property. Depending on the setup of the view controller, a view can be created using a Storyboard or a .xib file. You will not override this method unless you decide not to implement the view using Interface Builder.
viewDidLoad	This is called after the view is loaded. You will override this to perform additional adjustments to the user interface. You can set the text value of labels with the data received from a previous controller in the navigation hierarchy, for instance.
viewWillAppear	This is called just before the view is added to a view hierarchy. It is obviously called after viewDidLoad, and it may be called more than once during the view controller's life cycle.
viewDidAppear	This is called after the view is added to a view hierarchy. When this method is called, the view is visible, and its window property is no longer nil.
viewWillLayoutSubviews	This method is called when the view bounds change or are initialized and the view is about to lay out the subviews.
viewDidLayoutSubview	When this method is called, the bounds are set and the view has just called the layoutSubviews method.

The *appear-functions* are called when the controller is presented for the first time when a back button is pressed or a modal is closed, showing the underlying view controller again. If you override these methods, you are required to call them on super before executing your code.

Summary

With this chapter, you learned some of the very important basics that allow you to understand how UI elements are created, presented, and managed by the system. All these notions are essential to build simple and complex user interfaces, and they define a helpful starting point to easily read and appreciate the rest of this book.

The next chapter introduces the UIKit framework, an important set of classes that you will use in your everyday work. UIKit defines all the prebuilt UI elements of iOS and other classes that are fundamental to creating a complete and interactive layout.

2
UI Components Overview – UIKit

As with many other operative systems, iOS comes with its own UI library, UIKit, which is much more than a simple list of UI components. After reading the rest of this book, you'll realize that many topics are strictly connected to it—think of gestures, for instance. This chapter will be a basic overview of the main UI components provided by the framework; you'll learn how to use a component by adopting the most common properties and which functionalities you can work with while developing a user interface.

This chapter covers many different but related topics. Here is an overview of what you will read about in the next pages:

- Text elements and the keyboard
- Buttons, selectors, and user interaction
- View-based components
- A UI for structured data
- Custom components with the UIAppearance protocol

Exploring text elements

There are different ways to display text in iOS. You can draw strings directly in a graphic context through `NSString` or `NSAttributedString` or take advantage of the power of *Text Kit*, a framework dedicated to text drawing that is involved in all the controls we'll see in the next paragraphs. UIKit provides some really helpful classes built on Text Kit, which will simplify your work, allowing you not to worry about the way text is drawn. Let's go through all these classes.

Presenting text with UILabel

UILabel is a class that simply draws strings. Its text and attributedText properties define the text that is displayed by the label; the former receives a simple NSString instance to display plain text, while the latter receives an NSAttributedString instance to include styles, such as bold and italic, or draw strings with different colors and fonts:

The aspect of a label can be changed using dedicated properties:

- textColor: This is used for plain strings. It defines the color of the text with a UIColor instance.

- highlightedTextColor: This defines the color of the label when the highlighted property is set to true (for example, when you add a label inside a table cell and the cell is selected).

- textAlignment: This accepts an NSTextAlignment value to define the alignment of the text, such as Center, Left, or Justified.

- shadowColor-shadowOffset: This attaches a custom shadow to the label defined by color and offset with a CGSize value.

Labels are displayed on a single line by default. To allow the strings to be displayed on multiple lines, you have to set the numberOfLines property that, in conjunction with the lineBreakMode property, provides the needed information to split and truncate the text on more lines.

Here are some examples with different line-break modes:

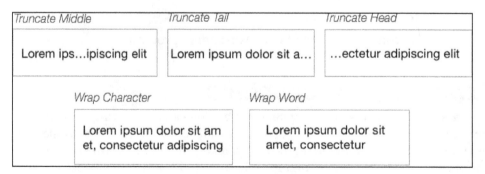

Starting with iOS8, the width of a multiline label can be automatically calculated through *Auto Layout* and defined by the `preferredMaxLayoutWidth` property. If you are supporting previous versions of iOS, you might need to define an explicit value for this property. The label's default font is *system font*, but it can be easily changed with the `font` property.

In some particular cases (or if you define an explicit width with `preferredMaxLayoutWidth`), the label bounds might not fit a string in its entirety. With the `adjustsFontSizeToFitWidth` property, you can set the font size to be decreased until the string is entirely visible inside the label bounds. With the `minimumScaleFactor` property, you can obtain a similar effect by defining, with a proportion, the minimum size to which the font can be reduced before the string gets truncated (for example, a font with size `24` and a minimum scale factor of `0.5` can be reduced up to a minimum value of `12`).

Receiving user input with UITextField

A text field is a control used to receive text inputs. The way users interact with this control is mainly handled by iOS; when a text field is selected, it becomes the *first responder*, and the system keyboard is automatically presented and starts listening for user input (more information about keyboards will be provided later in this chapter).

When a user is done with a text field, you can send `resignFirstResponder()` to the text field itself, and the keyboard will be automatically released. The selection of a text field can be forced through the `becomeFirstResponder()` function, which moves the focus on the text field when a user selects it.

For some properties, `UITextfield` instances are similar to labels. You can set and get the displayed text through `text` and `attributedText`, and you can also provide specific `textColor`, `font`, and `textAlignment` classes.

The text field draws text on a single line, and it can be plain or attributed text. If the `allowsEditingTextAttributes` property is set to true, a contextual menu with bold, italic, and underline styles selection is presented after a long press:

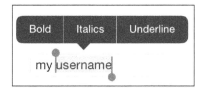

If the `placeholder` property is defined, this value is shown in place of text when the text field is empty. By default, the placeholder's color is light gray. The best way to set a custom placeholder is by defining the `attributedPlaceholder` property. As soon as the text field is selected, the placeholder text is removed.

The appearance of the text field can be modified through the `borderStyle` property, which accepts `UITextFieldBorderStyle` values such as `.None`, `.Line`, `.Bezel`, and `.RoundRect`. If the `.None` border style is chosen, you can provide the `background` and `disabledBackground` properties with one image, each to be used as a background. If the text field is disabled (meaning the `enable` property is equal to `false`), the second image is used.

Rounded Rect Border	Bezel Border
Username	Username
Line Border	Custom Background
Username	

You can go further with the customization by defining the `leftView` and `rightView` properties, which are two reserved views placed on the sides of the text field that add functionalities or specific information related to the current field content.

The visibility of these views is handled by two other properties—`leftViewMode` and `rightViewMode`—which require a `UITextFieldViewMode` value. They are strictly related to the text field's state. You can chose to never (`.Never`) show these views, always (`.Always`) show them, or present them while the user is editing (`.WhileEditing`) or not (`.UnlessEditing`).

With a really similar logic, by just defining the `clearViewMode` value, you can show a "clear" button to the right of the field that automatically removes the current content:

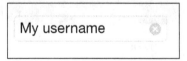

As for many other controls, a delegate handles and receives important information from the text fields; your controllers can implement the `UITextFieldDelegate` protocol that handles messages such as `textFieldDidBeginEditing:` when the user selects a text field and `textFieldShouldReturn:` when the user presses the "done" button on the keyboard. Some of these messages are also sent as notifications, so you can register an observer to handle specific text field changes.

Multiline text with UITextView

This class, which is a subclass of `UIScrollview`, is really similar to the text field, but it handles and displays multiple lines of text. A text view is typically used to display a large amount of text, such as the body of a document or a long message.

Some of its properties are the same that we listed for the `UITextField` class; you can, in fact, set and get the current `text` or `attributedText` class and define `textColor`, `font`, and `textAlignment`.

Lorem ipsum dolor sit er elit lamet,
consectetaur cillium adipisicing pecu,
sed do eiusmod tempor incididunt ut
labore et dolore magna aliqua. Ut
enim ad minim veniam, quis nostrud
exercitation ullamco laboris nisi ut
aliquip ex ea commodo consequat.
Duis aute irure dolor in reprehenderit
in voluptate velit esse cillum dolore eu
fugiat nulla pariatur. Excepteur sint
occaecat cupidatat non proident, sunt
in culpa qui officia deserunt mollit
anim id est laborum. Nam liber te
conscient to factor tum poen legum

Sometimes, you need to use a text view to show content that isn't editable by users. In this case, you can simply set the `editable` property to `false`. The text will be drawn using all the properties previously defined, but users won't be able to change the current content. It is possible to also prevent text selection by disabling the `selectable` property.

 When a text view is selected, it becomes the *first responder*, and the keyboard is automatically shown, just as for the text field.

A really interesting feature of `UITextView` instances is the ability to detect strings formatted as links, addresses, phone numbers, or events and automatically convert text into interactive elements that trigger actions when tapped. For example, if a user taps a phone number, an alert-style prompt displays a button that starts a call; if the number is long pressed, the user can choose to call the number, create a new contact, copy the string, or send a message to this number. Other examples are links opened with Safari, addresses opened with the Maps application, and events that can be added to the calendar.

You can choose which of these formats should be detected in the text view with the `dataDetectorTypes` property. Just note that in this case, the text view should be *selectable* but not *editable*.

These elements can be selected through Interface Builder or programmatically using a bitmask of `UIDataDetectorTypes` (for example, `.Link`, `.PhoneNumber`, `.CalendarEvent`, `.Address`, `.None`, and `.All`).

With the help of the Text Kit framework, we can perform some really complex operations on the text displayed in a text view. For example, we might want to add an image inside the text view while having the current text nicely wrapped around this image. An easy way to implement this layout is using the image frame to define an area that cannot contain text.

The code is straightforward, as follows:

```
var image = UIImageView(image: UIImage(named:"Image"))
self.textView.addSubview(image)
let exclusionPath = UIBezierPath(rect: image.frame)
self.textView.textContainer.exclusionPaths =
    [exclusionPath]
```

The image is attached as subview of the text view, and then an exclusion path is defined using `UIBezierPath` with the shape of `image.frame`. The last step is defining the exclusion paths for `textContainer`. As you can see in the following image, the text is drawn around the area occupied by the image frame:

Lorem ipsum dolor sit er elit lamet, consectetaur cillium adipisicing pecu, sed do eiusmod tempor incididunt ut labore et dolore magna aliqua. Ut enim ad minim veniam, quis nostrud exercitation ullamco

The main events taking place during the interaction with the text view can be handled by implementing `UITextViewDelegate`. The protocol defines methods such as `textViewDidBeginEditing:`, which tells the delegate that the editing has begun, and `textViewDidChangeSelection:`, which is triggered if the text view is selectable and the user highlights a portion of the text (the current selection can be retrieved using the `selectedRange` property).

Notes about the keyboard

When users interact with components such as text views or fields, these elements ask the system to display a keyboard to be able to receive user input.

The keyboard is a window that is independent from the user interface. This means that the keyboard just overlaps your UI without performing any automatic adjustments to the underlying views. You are, therefore, responsible for updating the UI so that it shows the appropriate elements in the available portion of the screen. You can already imagine that a really common issue occurs when the currently selected field gets overlapped by the keyboard.

There are different solutions that can help us fix this layout problem, but probably the easiest is to wrap UI elements inside `UIScrollView` and resize this view when the keyboard is displayed. We will discuss more about how to resize and move UI elements using Auto Layout in *Chapter 4, Auto Layout*.

 On iPad, the keyboard can be hidden and shown by the users with a button. However, it's an edge case, so it is a good choice to handle the layout without requiring the user to manually change the keyboard visibility in order to display the underlying content.

Keyboard events

You can subscribe to some useful notifications triggered by the system to be notified of keyboard events. Take a look at the following table:

Notification	Description
• `UIKeyboardWillShowNotification` • `UIKeyboardDidShowNotification`	These notifications are posted just before (and after) the keyboard is presented on screen. From the notification's `userInfo` dictionary, you can get useful information about the keyboard. Using the `UIKeyboardFrameEndUserInfoKey` key, for example, you can retrieve the end frame of the keyboard in the screen coordinates.
• `UIKeyboardWillHideNotification` • `UIKeyboardDidHideNotification`	These notifications are posted just before (and after) the keyboard is dismissed.
• `UIKeyboardWillChangeFrame Notification` • `UIKeyboardDidChangeFrame Notification`	These notifications are posted just before (and after) the keyboard frame changes. An example might be when a user drags the undocked keyboard up and down on iPad.

Keyboard configuration

To help users type any input, the keyboard can be configured to better fit the kind of data the text field expects. As both `UITextField` and `UITextView` implement the `UITextInputTraits` protocol, you can define some properties that adjust the keyboard behavior and its appearance. You can also completely change the type of the keyboard with the `keyboardType` property that receives a `UIKeyboardType` value, such as `NumberPad`, `URL`, `EmailAddress`, and even `Twitter`. Depending on the selected type, the keyboard's layout changes to show only the useful keys.

Other useful configurations are `keyboardAppearance`, which alters the color of the keyboard (you have only two choices here: `dark` or `light`), and `returnType`, which helps you set the label of the return type by picking one among the available options such as `Go, Done, Next,` and `Google`.

Exploring buttons and selectors

UIKit provides a great list of components that you can include in your user interfaces to intercept user input. Most of the UI elements you will see in this section are based on the `UIControl` class, and their main role is to convert touch events into actions or choices. How the user interacts with a control depends on the type of the control itself.

There are simple buttons that can be tapped to trigger an action, for instance, or controls that accept drag and drop—think sliders or switches—to set a value. Don't worry if you don't find the control that fits your needs. Later in this book (*Chapter 8, How to Build Custom Controls*, specifically), you will learn how to implement a completely custom control. You'll notice that just as for the default controls, the starting point will be the `UIControl` class.

UIButton and user interaction

The `UIButton` class defines generic buttons that intercept the user's tap. You can create different types of buttons with the `buttonWithType` class function, which receives `UIButtonType` as the input. `System` buttons are automatically highlighted when pressed, whereas `Custom` buttons present the button without any other information about the interaction.

A short list of built-in buttons with predefined images is at your disposal to help you build standard user interfaces.

Default button	Add Contact	Detail disclosure	Info
Button	(+)	(i)	(i)

A button can be defined with a title, title color, attributed title, title shadow, image, and background (which can itself be an image or a color). These properties are associated with a state (`UIControlState`) that identifies the current state of the button: `.Normal` (when the button is not pressed), `.Highlighted` (when it is), and `.Disabled`.

You can configure all these properties for one or more states; the button is automatically updated with your choices when the `state` variable changes. It is important to note that you cannot set a generic value for these properties; they have to be defined through a state. For example, if you want to set a title, you need to write:

```
button.setTitle("The Title", forState: .Normal)
```

The other way around, you can access the current value using the `current<propertyName>` getter (for example, `currentTitle`) that returns the value for the current state.

You don't have to define a value for all the states, though. What happens most of the time is that you set a value for the `Normal` state, and then this setting is used for all the other states, except for those that are explicitly defined with a different value.

Under the hood, a button draws its title with `UILabel` and its image using a `UIImageView`. These properties are read-only, but their internal properties can, in turn, be accessed to further customize the button's look. You can change the font of `titleLabel` through its `font` property, for example, as follows:

```
button.titleLabel?.font = UIFont.systemFontOfSize(12)
```

The target-action pattern

While you'll learn more about the `UIControl` subclasses in *Chapter 8, How to Build Custom Controls*, we can now introduce the concept of the target-action pattern that is used by most of the controls that we will analyze in these pages. This pattern defines how a control can request the execution of a function (*action*) to another object (*target*) in response to an event.

This pattern, just as an example, is used by `UIButton` instances to call a function when a button is pressed. As you'll learn in the next chapter, a common way to connect a button to an action is through Storyboard, but you can also obtain the same result programmatically with the `addTarget:action:forControlEvent` function, as in the following code:

```
button.addTarget(self, action: "buttonPressed:",
forControlEvents: .TouchUpInside)
```

This function is really important because it is used by all the main controls to connect an event to the execution of an action. These events are defined by the `UIControlEvent` structure. In the previous example, a button requests the `buttonPressed:` function on the current view controller after a user lifts his/her finger off the button. The `buttonPressed` function receives the sender of the action, which is the button itself. Now, take a look at the following script:

```
func buttonPressed(sender:UIButton){
    var title = sender.titleForState(.Normal)!
    print("\(title) button pressed!")
}
```

Boolean selection with UISwitch

A switch is a really simple control that has only two possible states: *on* or *off*. To change the current state, a user can simply tap the control or drag its handle. As soon as the value changes, the `UIControlEventValueChanged:` event is generated, and just as it happens for `UIButton`, you can intercept this event with a target-action pattern via Storyboard or programmatically by executing the following code:

```
// Set the target-action
aSwitch.addTarget(self, action: "valueChanged:", forControlEvents:
.ValueChanged)
...
func switchValueChanged(aSwitch:UISwitch){
print("value is \(aSwitch.on)")
}
```

The current value of the switch can be retrieved and set using the on property, which is, quite predictably, `true` if the switch is on. If you want to set the on state by performing an animation, you can call the `setOn(_:animated:)` function.

Control customization

As you'll note at the end of the chapter, the appearance of most of the `UIControl` subclasses can be customized through some specific function. For the `UISwitch` instances, we can set `onTintColor:` to define the background of the switch when the value is "on", use `tint` to set the border color of the control when value is "off", and fiddle with `thumbTintColor` to colorize the thumb element.

Selecting values with UISlider

A slider is a control used to select a value within a range of `Float` values. Users interact with the slider by dragging the thumb element horizontally over the slider area. The slider has a `minimumValue` of *0.0* and a `maximumValue` of *1.0*, by default. These values can be changed, depending on your needs, to positive and negative numbers.

The current value can be set and retrieved through the `value` property, and, not unlike the `UISwitch`, as soon as the value is changed by the user, the `UIControlEventValueChanged` event is triggered. By setting the `continuous` property to `false`, you can choose to trigger the "value changed" event only when the user leaves the thumb; otherwise, it will be constantly triggered while the user is dragging if the property is set to `true`.

Sometimes, it is useful to force the slider to work with `Int` values instead of `Float`. You can do this with the action function by simply rounding the current value to the subsequent integer, as you can note in the following lines of code:

```
func sliderValueChanged(slider:UISlider){
    var roundedValue = Int(slider.value + 0.5)
    slider.value = Float(roundedValue)
    println("Slider value \(slider.value)")
}
```

Control customization

The slider can be thoroughly customized. You can set the track color with the `tintColor` property or even define a color for the track area to the left (`minimumTrackTintColor`) and right (`maximumTrackTintColor`) of the thumb. The thumb color can be customized too, using the `thumbTintColor` property.

As if this is not enough, you can completely change the appearance of the slider using custom images for the track and for the thumb, depending on the current state, through `setMinimum/MaximumTrackImage(_:forState:)` and `setThumbImage(_:forState:)`. Other decorations that can be added to the slider are two images placed to the left and right of the slider through `minimum/maximumValueImage`.

User choices through UISegmentedControl

The segmented control is a set of multiple buttons that allows the selection of a specific value among multiple predefined choices:

You can get the number of segments through the `numberOfSegments` property and for each segment you can define a title (`setTitle:forSegmentAtIndex:`) or an image (`setImage:forSegmentAtIndex:`). Each segment width is identical to the other if the `apportionsSegmentWidthsByContent` property is `false`, otherwise segment widths will vary depending on their content. Width can also be forced with `setWidth:forSegmentAtIndex:`.

The default behavior for this control is allowing the user to select a single segment and keep it selected. You can change this behavior by setting the `momentary` property to `true`. The segment tapped by user will now be highlighted for a short time, and then it will be automatically deselected.

You have two different ways to work with the selected value:

- The first is the target-action pattern, which works exactly the same on the segmented control. You can intercept changes on the selected value through the `UIControlEventValueChanged` trigger, just as we saw before.

- As another option, you can get the selected value later through the `selectedSegmentIndex` property, which returns the selected index (starting from `0`). If no segment is selected, this property is equal to `UISegmentedControlNoSegment`.

The segments that will be part of the control can be easily defined through the Storyboard; alternatively, if you need, they can be added or removed at runtime using the `insertSegmentWith<Title/Image>:atIndex:animated:`, `removeSegmentAtIndex:animated:`, or `removeAllSegments` methods.

Control customization

You can configure the style of the segmented control, just as we did for the other controls. The main color can be defined through `tintColor`, and as a consequence, it will set the borders and background color of the selected index.

You can also change the style of the segment more dramatically using custom images. As the segmented control is dependent on bar metrics (the bars have different sizes on iPhone with landscape orientation), you can define the images for each metric.

The images you can customize are the background for the segments and the dividers for each combination of states. The following example gives you an idea of what you can do:

```
// Background for Normal and Selected state
segment.setBackgroundImage(bg,forState: UIControlState.Normal,
    barMetrics: .Default)
segment.setBackgroundImage(bg_sel,forState:
  UIControlState.Selected,
    barMetrics: .Default)

// Dividers for some combination of states
segment.setDividerImage(div_nor_nor,
    forLeftSegmentState: .Normal,
    rightSegmentState: .Normal, barMetrics: .Default)
segment.setDividerImage(div_nor_sel,
    forLeftSegmentState: .Normal,
    rightSegmentState: .Selected, barMetrics: .Default)
segment.setDividerImage(div_sel_nor,
    forLeftSegmentState: .Selected,
    rightSegmentState: .Normal, barMetrics: .Default)
```

Here, you can see the result of this code and the single images used for the background and state combinations:

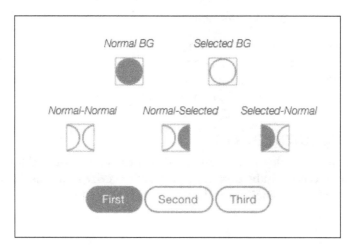

Selecting values with UIPickerView and UIDatePicker

Pickers are UI elements that are useful to display long lists of choices grouped in one or more spinning wheels, also called **components**. Users can easily interact with this control just by rotating the wheels.

Before diving into the functionality of the picker let's introduce how a picker view structure is structured.

As we've discussed previously, a picker view consists of different components (the wheels). Each wheel is assigned to an index location, and *0* is the value for the leftmost of them. The elements in the wheels are defined in one or more *rows* that are, in turn, assigned to indexes starting from *0*, which finally contain the actual content.

In order to define the structure of a picker view, you need to configure a data source (`UIPickerViewDataSource`) and delegate (`UIPickerViewDelegate`), which are responsible for the definition of the picker's content and respond to triggered events.

Here is a list of the main functions of these protocols needed to configure and handle a picker: data source and delegate methods.

Data source methods return the information needed to set the content of the picker. Take a look:

Data source method	Description
`numberOfComponentsInPickerView:`	This returns an integer that identifies the number of the needed components/wheels. The only parameter of this function is the current picker view that, in case you are presenting more than one picker in your UI, is relevant in helping you distinguish which picker you are configuring.

Data source method	Description
`pickerView: numberOfRowsInComponent:`	This defines the number of rows that each wheel has to show. With this function, you receive the current picker and, obviously, the component for which you are defining the number of rows.

Delegate methods are handy to intercept picker events and configure some really specific layout information. Take a look at the following table:

Delegate method	Description
`pickerView:<content>ForRow:forComponent:` (Where `<content>` can be title, attributedString or view)	This set of functions returns content that will be displayed at a specific component-row combination. You can easily define it with `String` or `AttributedString`. In this case, a label displayed in the system font is automatically created for each row. You can customize the look of the rows by defining content with a totally custom view.
`pickerView:didSelectRow:inComponent:`	This function is called when a row is selected. To be even more precise, it is called as soon as a wheel stops moving and the user's touch event ends.
`pickerView:widthForComponent:`	With this function, you can suggest the width for each single component. Depending on the configuration and content, the final result may vary from the value that you return here. Note that the height of a picker is fixed, and you can assign only one value: `162`, `180`, or `216`.
`pickerView:rowHeightForComponent:`	Here, you can pass the height of the rows for each component to the picker.

`UIDatePicker` internally uses a picker view to allow users to select date and time. Depending on the `datePickerMode` property, you can allow selection of time (`Time`), date (`Date`), and date and time (`DateAndTime`) values or display a countdown (`CountDownTimer`).

The order and value of the wheels are defined by `datePickerMode` and the date localization, which can be set with the `calendar` and `locale` properties.

The current date value can be set and retrieved from the date property, and as you don't set a delegate on a date picker, if you need to intercept the "value changed" trigger, you have to add an observer on the UIControlEventValueChanged event.

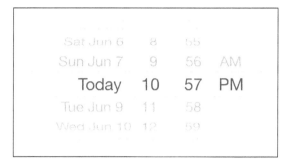

 A date picker cannot be customized at all; you cannot even change the font used by the rows. The only way to obtain a custom date picker is to work with a default picker view and implement all the date/time logics yourself.

Updating values with UIStepper

A stepper is an element that's useful to easily increase and decrease a numeric value through a guided interface. The predefined interface presents just two buttons with the minus "-" and plus "+" symbols, and its layout is really similar to a segmented control with just two segments.

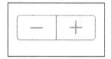

The current value can be accessed through the value property, and if the autorepeat property is true, it can be increased/decreased continuously just by keeping the plus or minus button pressed. The increase or decrease steps are defined by the stepValue property, which defines how the value changes with every step.

The minimumValue and maximumValue (that are both Double) automatically define the range of possible values. If the wrap property is equal to true when the maximum (or minimum) value is reached, the current value automatically becomes equal to the minimum (or maximum) value.

If you want to intercept the "value changed" event, you have to register for the UIControlEventValueChanged event, just as for the other controls.

Control customization

The stepper can be customized with functions that are really similar to those used to customize the segmented control.

The background for the buttons can be defined with the `setBackgroundImage:forState:` function by setting images for the possible `UIControlState` values, such as `Normal` and `Highlighted`. The divider image between the two buttons can be customized with the `setDividerImage:forLeftSeg ment State:rightSegmentState:` function.

You can also set custom images for the plus and minus symbols, depending on the current state, by calling the `set<Decrement/Increment>ImageForState:` functions.

View-based components

The following controls are subclasses of `UIView`, and they are useful to display noninteractive information or act as containers.

Showing progress with UIProgressView

A progress view is an indicator of progress over time. You can see an example of this control during downloads or when sending an e-mail from the Mail app:

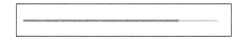

This control is extremely simple. The only property you need to set and read is `progress`, a value between `0.0` and `1.0`. When this value is `0.0`, the progress bar is empty, while it is full when its value is equal to `1.0`. You can perform a simple animation if you set the progress value using the `setProgress:animated:` function and passing `true` for the animated parameter.

Control customization

The control can be easily customized with dedicated functions. You can customize the track that is not filled by specifying a tint with the `trackTintColor:` function or even using an image with the `trackImage:` function. The same customizations are available for the progress bar through the `progressTintColor:` and `progressImage:` functions.

Working with UIActivityIndicatorView

When views are loading — for example, while waiting for content to be retrieved from remote APIs — it is really important to give feedback to users by informing them that the UI is not frozen; in fact, quite the opposite, it's waiting for some other events to be completed.

The activity indicator view is exactly what you need to give this immediate feedback. This component is just an easy spinning wheel that you can place in your UI while some other operations are running.

The animation of the wheel can be handled by the `startAnimating` and `stopAnimating` functions, and you can automatically hide the wheel when the animation is stopped by setting the `hidesWhenStopped` property.

Control customization

This control has only a few possible customizable properties. You can define the wheel tint with the `color` property or set the style of the wheel with the `activityIndicatorViewStyle` property that accepts these predefined styles: `WhiteLarge`, `White`, and `Gray`.

Introducing UIImageView and UIImage

An image view is a container for static or animated images. It works in conjunction with the `UIImage` class, which shows an image in one of the following formats: JPEG, PNG, TIFF, GIF, DIB, a Windows icon, a Windows cursor, and a XWindow bitmap. The image can be read from the application bundle and initialized by name with the `init(named:)` function, or it can be created on the fly by downloading its data from a remote source and converting this data into a `UIImage` object with the `init(data:)` function, for example.

Different versions of the same images should be provided to fit different screen pixel densities. You can address the images for a specific screen by using suffixes in their filenames. For instance, with `@2x`, you assign a `scale` property of `2.0` (suited to standard Retina displays), and with `@3x`, the `scale` property is `3.0` (suitable for 5.5-inch screens, such as that of iPhone 6 Plus).

A handy way to manage different image versions is using an *asset catalog* (by default, Xcode creates the *images.xcassets* catalog for every new project), in which you only need to drag and drop images with the right resolutions. There are dedicated slots for the 1x, 2x, and 3x versions and even more options if you want to target specific devices, such as iPad or Apple Watch, or specific orientations:

An asset catalog handles different image sizes using *trait collections*. You'll learn more about traits in *Chapter 5*, *Adaptive User Interfaces*; for now, it suffices to say that the `UIImageAsset` class stores all the image versions provided by the asset catalog and returns the best image format, depending on the current device type and orientation.

A `UIImage` instance has some interesting properties that define how the image is drawn. You can set the *rendering mode* image by initializing it with the `imageWithRenderingMode:` method and force the image to always be drawn as original (`AlwaysOriginal`) or as a template (`AlwaysTemplate`). The latter is useful for any single-color images that you can tint with any color, depending on your UI's needs. The `AlwaysOriginal` mode, instead, forces the image to be drawn without drawing modifications in the system.

Another interesting feature that alters the way an image is drawn is related to *cap insets*. The `resizableImageWithCapInsets:` initializer returns an image that can be easily resized by keeping the corners of the image fixed in their state and creating resizable areas that can be seamlessly repeated along the entire image's width or length. Here is an example to show you how the cap insets work:

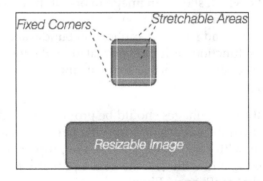

An image view is initialized with the displayed image with the `init(image:)` method, while a supplementary image can be provided through the `init(image:highlightedImage:)` function. If the `highlighted` property of the image view is true, the highlighted image is shown instead of the default image.

As `UIImageView` is a subclass of `UIView`, it inherits all of its properties and methods, similar to `clipToBounds`, which was discussed in the previous chapter, and `contentMode`. This property is really important because it defines how the image is drawn inside the image view's bounds. By default, it is scaled to fill the bound's area (`scaleToFill`).

This option doesn't respect the aspect ratio of the image, though, stretching it to fill the entire area if necessary. Other options can totally change the drawing behavior. You can scale the image while keeping the aspect ratio (`scaleAspectFill` or `scaleAspectFit`), for example, or just draw the image at its original size at the center of the image view (`center`).

Introducing UIScrollView

Scroll views are complex elements, and an exhaustive description of this class would require an entire chapter by itself. Let's just introduce this control by describing some of its properties and the way you should integrate it in your UIs.

A scroll view comes in handy when you need to display content that is bigger than its container. This control acts as a mask and manages all the needed logics to allow users to scroll and zoom in on the content inside this container. Under the hood, the origin of the content is adjusted in response to the user's gestures, and it is subsequently moved inside the container by updating `contentOffset`. The container then clips the content, which remains outside its frame. With the following image, you can better understand how the content is masked by the scroll view and how only a portion of the content is displayed:

The scroll view needs to know the size of the content it is displaying to calculate the scrolling area. Sometimes, the content you want to put inside a scroll view is composed of different elements, so it's not easy to identify an accurate content size. In this case, an easy technique to set up the scroll view's content is to embed all the views into a single parent view and then, with Auto Layout, set width, height, and constraints to place it inside the scroll view.

It is important to know that in order to calculate the scroll area, a scroll view needs all of its four sides to be tied to valid constraints. Moving further with our approach, we can just tie the four sides of the parent view to the four sides of the scroll view (you'll learn all you need to know about Auto Layout in *Chapter 4, Auto Layout*).

When a user starts scrolling, the horizontal and vertical scroll bars are displayed. You can hide these elements with the `show<Horizontal/Vertical>ScrollIndicator:` properties or change their styles (black or white) by setting `indicatorStyle`. You can even temporarily disable scrolling with the `scrollEnabled` property.

An interesting way to interact with a scroll view is implementing the `UIScrollViewDelegate` protocol. With this protocol, you can intercept a lot of information about user interactions, similar to `scrollViewDidScroll:`, when the scrolling is finished, or `scrollViewWillBeginDecelerating:`, when the user lifts his/her finger after scrolling and the deceleration of the scroll view starts.

Another set of important properties is related to the zoom action. If you want to allow users to perform content zoom with a pinch gesture, you need to set `minimumZoomScale` and `maximumZoomScale` in order to define the range within which the scroll view contents will be scaled. At this point, you have to implement the `viewForZoomingInScrollView:` delegate method, which returns the view that you want to zoom.

Considering that you'll typically want to zoom the entire scroll view's content, if you implement the content structure with a single parent view as we suggested before, you should return this view. Every time a user performs a pinch over the scroll view, the content will be scaled by a value that is proportional to the pinch distance and stored in the `zoomScale` property.

Managing and presenting structured data

When there's a lot of information to be shown in a single view, you can rely on specific controls that are optimized for this very task: the table and collection views.

Introducing UITableView

A table view displays a list of *cells* through a vertical scrollable layout. All the items presented by a table view can be grouped in *sections*, and some supplementary information, such as *headers* and *footer*, can be attached to the UI to improve the readability of the information.

`UITableView` is a subclass of `UIScrollView` and inherits all the functionalities from this class.

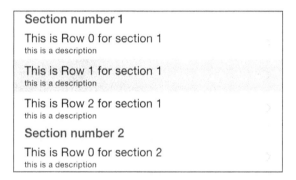

The cells presented by a table are instances of `UITableViewCell` (or its subclasses). You can use some prebuilt cell types that are provided by the system (basic, right detail, left detail, and subtitle) and end up being very useful if you just want to display simple information. Alternatively, you can build your own cell styles so that they can accommodate any type of information your data may need.

The cell drawing process is heavily optimized through a cell *registration/de-queuing* procedure. Cell classes are registered through the `registerClass:forCellReuseId entifier:` function that connects a reuse identifier to a `UITableViewCell` subclass. From now on, before creating a new cell, you can use the `dequeueReusableCellWit hIdentifier:forIndexPath:` function to check whether a cell with the same reuse identifier is available in the current reuse queue and use this cell instead of creating a new one.

Cells that are removed from screen are candidates for the reuse queue. To better understand how this optimization improves performance, imagine a table with 3000 rows; thanks to the reuse queue, we will only handle around 10 cells in our device's memory instead of all 3000.

When you define a table cell using the Storyboard, you can set up a reuse identifier that will be automatically registered without the need to call the `registerNib:forCellReuseIdentifier:` or `registerClass:forCellReuseIdentifier:` function.

The data displayed with a table view is provided through a *data source* object that implements `UITableViewDataSource`. This object has to implement some required methods that are needed to set the minimum information for the table, as follows:

Method	Description
`tableView:numberOfRowsInSection:`	This returns an integer that represents the number of rows for the specified section. You can also implement the `numberOfSectionsInTableView:` function to define the number of sections. The default value for sections is 1.
`tableView:cellForRowAtIndexPath:`	This method is responsible for building and returning a cell for a specific index path. Keep in mind that the index path is an instance of the `NSIndexPath` class, and it uses the `row` and `section` properties to identify the cell that the system requires.

An extremely simple example of code for an object that implements the data source protocol is as follows:

```
func tableView(tableView: UITableView,
numberOfRowsInSection section: Int) -> Int {
return 10
}

func tableView(tableView: UITableView,
cellForRowAtIndexPath indexPath: NSIndexPath) -> UITableViewCell {

var cell = tableView.dequeueReusableCellWithIdentifier("MyCell")
as!MYCustomTableViewCell
    cell.customTitle = "Row \(indexPath.row)"

    return cell
}
```

A table view can also interact with a *delegate* object that implements the UITableViewDelegate protocol to handle cell selections, intercept table edit events, and configure headers and footers.

A typical example of a delegate is a table that presents a list of elements that a user can select to access a detail view for each element. The delegate object might implement the tableView:didSelectRowAtIndexPath: function, which includes all the logics needed to present the next view with details regarding the selected object.

Introducing UICollectionView

The other control you might want to adopt to display long lists of items is the collection view. The main difference between the collection and table views is that with the collection view, you can customize quite dramatically the way that items are displayed. In fact, you can easily obtain grids of items (for instance, row-by-row presentations similar to table views) or even create completely custom layouts.

The items displayed by a collection view are UICollectionViewCell instances, and in line with what happens for the table view, they can be grouped in *sections*. In addition to cells, a collection view might present two other kinds of views: the *decoration view* and the *supplementary view*. The former isn't related to the content (it might be used for backgrounds, for instance), while the latter is used to draw elements such as section headers and footers.

A collection view is also similar to a table view in the way it defines its data. `UICollectionViewDataSource` is responsible for providing the contents displayed by the collection through methods such as `collectionView:numberOfItemsInSec tion:` and `collectionView:cellForItemAtIndexPath:`. As you can see, these are really similar to the methods implemented by a table view data source.

Cells and supplementary views are subclasses of `UICollectionReusableView`, and the collection view presents these kinds of views with the registration and de-queuing process we saw before. You can register the class or a nib using `registe rClass:forCellWithReuseIdentifier:` / `registerNib:forCellWithReuseIdent ifier:` (or their supplementary view versions), and then, rather then creating a new instance for these views every time, you can use `dequeueReusableCellWithReuseI dentifier:forIndexPath:` to retrieve a cell that was previously queued (for example, after a cell goes offscreen)—same as with table views.

A *delegate* object that implements the `UICollectionViewDelegate` protocol can handle useful events triggered by the collection view, such as the selection of a cell (`collectionView:didSelectItemAtIndexPath:`).

If you create a collection view using a Storyboard, `UICollectionViewFlowLayout` is used as the layout of the collection by default. This layout shows the items in a grid that can be customized through parameters such as `itemSize`, `minimumLineSpacing`, and `minimumInteritemSpacing`. This is a good choice that is suitable for many use cases, but what makes a collection view so interesting is the fact that you can create a heavily customized layout by subclassing `UICollectionViewLayout`.

The UIAppearance protocol

If there's one thing the controls we've talked about so far have in common, it is that they can be graphically customized with the use of simple functions. This is a great a feature that has been added to UIKit since iOS5, and it allows us to modify the looks of any default control with just a few lines of code.

This feature is improved by the `UIAppearance` protocol that, thanks to the *appearance proxy*, forwards the customizations to all the instances of a specific class. The appearance proxy for a class can be retrieved using the `appearance` function, and as it returns `instancetype`, its properties can be easily accessed. Here is an example of the code needed to set `onTintColor` for all the `UISwitch` instances of an application:

```
UISwitch.appearance().onTintColor = UIColor.redColor()
```

The properties that take part in the UIAppearance protocol and can therefore be modified through the appearance proxy must be marked with the UI_APPEARANCE_ SELECTOR tag. This portion of the original definition of the onTintColor property from the UISwitch.h file confirms this:

```
... UIColor *onTintColor UI_APPEARANCE_SELECTOR;
```

You can also specify which of the instances for the class will receive the customization using refined versions of the appearance function: appearanceWhenContainedIn: allows you to get only the instances that are contained within a specific container, such as UINavigationBar or UIToolBar, while appearanceForTraitCollection: returns the appearance proxy for the specified trait collection.

Hands-on code

The example code for this chapter is all about UI customization! You'll learn how to customize the UISlider class using custom images and the UIAppearance proxy. The final result will be a UISlider class that is completely customized, similar to the following:

Open the start project for *Chapter 2, UI Components Overview – UIKit*. Select Images. xcassets to create the needed images. The catalog asset should already contain one asset called AppIcon. Create a new asset by clicking on the + symbol and select **New Image Asset**. A new empty image asset will be created. Double-click on the new asset to rename it minTrack. At this point, if you select it, you should see three available slots on your right: 1x, 2x, and 3x.

These are the slots where the images to be used to customize the minTrack property should be dragged and dropped. Open the assets folder that you can find in the source code for this chapter and just drag the minTrack.png, minTrack@2x.png, and minTrack@3x.png images to the relative slots (you don't have to drag the images one by one; just select all the three images and drop them over any of the slots).

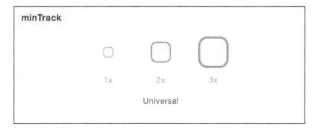

Repeat the previous steps for the `maxTrack` and `thumb` images.

Now, you can finally write code that's necessary to configure the custom element of the slider, as follows:

```
let minTrack = UIImage(named: "minTrack")
let maxTrack = UIImage(named: "maxTrack")
let thumb = UIImage(named: "thumb")

// Create resizable images
let resizableMinTrack =
minTrack?.resizableImageWithCapInsets(
UIEdgeInsets(top: 0, left: 5, bottom: 0, right: 5))

let resizableMaxTrack =
maxTrack?.resizableImageWithCapInsets(
UIEdgeInsets(top: 0, left: 5, bottom: 0, right: 5))

// Configure the styles!
UISlider.appearance().setMaximumTrackImage(
resizableMaxTrack, forState: UIControlState.Normal)

UISlider.appearance().setMinimumTrackImage(
resizableMinTrack, forState: UIControlState.Normal)

UISlider.appearance().setThumbImage(
thumb, forState: UIControlState.Normal)
```

The first part of the code initializes images that are then transformed into resizable elements thanks to the `imageWithCapInsets` function.

Lastly, the appearance proxy for the UISlider class is used to set custom images for the `minimumTrack`, `maximumTrack`, and `thumb` properties. From now on, when you create a new instance of `UISlider`, these customizations will be used.

Summary

In this chapter, we went through a long list of components provided by UIKit. Keep in mind that UIKit is not just a library of UI elements, and it covers many other interesting topics, such as gestures, UI dynamics, and application structures such as navigation and tab bar controllers.

In the next chapter, we'll go over the concept of Storyboard with the help of some practical examples. Along the way, you'll also find out how to initialize some of the controls that we saw in the previous pages.

3
Interface Builder, XIB, and Storyboard

Apple provides a complete list of tools to simplify and improve the way we build applications. Xcode, by all means, can be considered a big container of these tools.

One of the Xcode instruments that you will use the most is the Interface Builder editor. During this chapter, you'll learn how it can be employed to create interfaces dropping components into a Storyboard (or an XIB file) and how those components can be connected to your classes.

Interface Builder

Information about user interfaces is stored in dedicated files; in fact, one or more *Storyboards* could potentially include the interface for the entire application and all navigation logics. We'll discuss this in more detail later in the chapter. An **XML Interface Builder** (**XIB**) file, on the other hand, is normally used to contain the interface of a single view (or portions of it). In some ways, you can imagine a Storyboard as a set of XIB files connected through navigation information.

Both Storyboards and XIB files are XML files that are compiled into *Nib packages* at build time. Interface Builder is a visual editor that reads and edits the information contained in XML files; it translates the XML into a visual representation of the views it describes and converts any updates that come from the editor into XML in turn.

Working with the XML format is extremely practical because any versioning control system can easily perform different operations. You could even manually update the XML and have Interface Builder automatically read your updates (you are not encouraged to do so, however).

An overview of the editor

As soon as you open a `.storyboard` or `.xib` file, Xcode presents you with the Interface Builder editor:

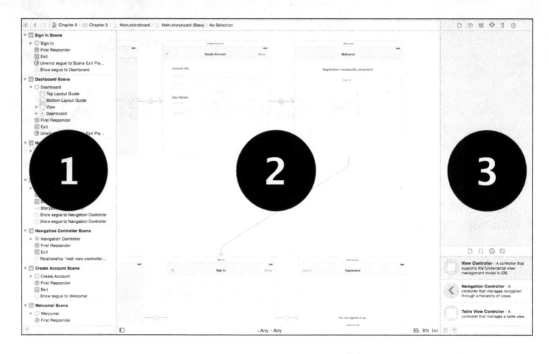

You can easily notice three different areas marked with numbers in the preceding image. They represent the following:

1. The document outline contains a tree structure that represents all the view controllers and elements available in the Storyboard/XIB file. It is a handy way to select specific elements, especially when the user interface is crowded with different components.

2. In the center of the screen, you can see the interface editor. From this area, you can create new view controllers, place and move elements inside views, define navigation flows, and connect UI components to your classes.

3. The utilities panel allows you to add details to the UI elements: you need to first select an element from the interface editor or document outline, and then you can access and set all the element properties through six different subsections of the utilities panel:

Let's take a look at the different options that we have here from left to right:

File inspector	This panel is related to the whole Storyboard/XIB file and not to the single UI component. It not only shows all the information about the XML file (such as its location in your computer), but also allows you to specify localizations and inclusion in targets.
Quick Help	When a component is selected, this panel gives an overview of the appropriate documentation.
Identity inspector	This allows you to edit the identity of the selected components, defining their custom classes and managing runtime attributes. From this view, you can also get the *object ID* of the selected component used inside XML files to identify the element itself.
Attributes inspector	This panel changes depending on the current selection, showing the editable attributes of the current component.
Size inspector	All the information about bounds and frames for the selected element and all its Auto Layout constraints are accessible from this section.
Connections inspector	This panel presents an overview of all the connections available for the selected component. For UIButton, for instance, you will see all UIControlEvents available and the actions connected to them.

At the bottom of this panel, you can access another list of four subsections:

The first two are not strictly related to user interface. The first button lets you quickly access a list of template files that you can drag and drop inside the **Project** inspector, while the second shows a list of editable code snippets.

The last two buttons are, on the other hand, very useful when working with Storyboards and XIB files, allowing access to the *objects library*, which contains all the components that you can drag and drop into the UI, and the *media library*, which lists all the images available for your project.

Working with XIB files

Even if an XIB file can be used in different ways, its most common use is defining the interface of a single-view controller.

When you create a new view controller, you can flag the choice **Also create XIB file** to automatically associate an XIB file to the new view controller:

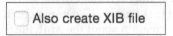

When you open the XIB file with the interface editor, you'll see that the document outline already contains some elements:

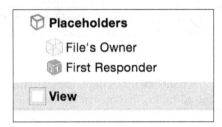

The **Placeholders** section includes two proxy objects that you most likely won't need to update. The **File's Owner** section describes the class that will own the interface created through the XIB file. In this case, this object represents the view controller class that you create with the XIB file. If you haven't used the wizard to create the XIB file, you need to set up this element manually from the **Identity** inspector, filling the **Class** field with the name of the class that you want as the owner of this interface.

The **First Responder** section is a proxy to any object that, at any given time during the application's execution, has the first responder status. For example, when a user selects a text field, the first responder proxy object points to it.

The document outline already contains a *view* object. This view is really important because it will be the container of the interface that you will build. If the XIB file is created alongside a view controller, the view will already be connected to the main view of the file's owner (the view controller itself). You can verify this connection by selecting the view from the outline and checking the **Connections** inspector.

From now on, every time a view controller instance is created using the init(coder:) method, the view controller's view property will point to the view defined in the XIB file.

Instantiating a view controller with a specific XIB file is really simple thanks to the init(nibName:bundle:) initializer that takes the XIB filename as the parameter. Take a look at the following code:

```
let signInVC = SignInViewController
    (nibName:"SignInViewController",  bundle:nil)
```

Managing user interfaces with Storyboards

A Storyboard can be considered a container of XIB files that can be connected through navigation logics. You can also use more than one Storyboard to organize view controllers in different groups. For example, you can have a Storyboard that manages all the view controllers for the settings of an application and another to handle the application's core.

Each Storyboard has an entry point controller called *initial view controller* that defines where the navigation starts. It is used by the application's launch process described in *Chapter 1, UI Fundamentals*, to define which controller of the main Storyboard to show when the application starts. The initial view controller is visually highlighted with a gray arrow pointing to the left of the view controller. To set the preferred initial view controller, you can manually move the arrow from another controller or check the voice "is initial view controller" in the **Attributes** inspector.

Connecting user interfaces with your code

Putting a new element inside your interface files is extremely simple. You just have to select one of the available objects from the objects library and drag and drop it inside the interface editor.

For example, let's say you want to create the user interface for a subclass of `UIViewController` called `SignInViewController` that implements user sign-in. The first step is to *drag and drop a view controller* object inside the Storyboard interface editor. Then, select the newly added view controller, and from the **Identity** inspector (third button on the right-hand side panel), update the information of the *custom class area*, specifying the name `SignInViewController` as the class name. The view controller you see inside the interface editor is now an instance of this class, and you can draw and *connect* the necessary *elements and methods*.

In the `SignInViewController` class, you defined the *username* and *password* text fields and the `signIn` method. The two text fields can be created inside the interface editor with a simple *drag and drop*. It is now necessary to expose the two text fields from the class file to Interface Builder, prefixing their definitions with the `@IBOutlet` keyword, as follows:

```
@IBOutlet weak var usernameTextField:UITextField!
@IBOutlet weak var passwordTextField:UITextField!
```

A connection between the user interface elements and class properties can be easily achieved from the document outline by simply *pressing the Ctrl key* and *dragging* from the view controller icon to the text fields. When you release the mouse button, a new window will appear and allow you to *select* the property you want to connect to the user interface element. You can verify that the element is connected from the connection editor on the utilities panel.

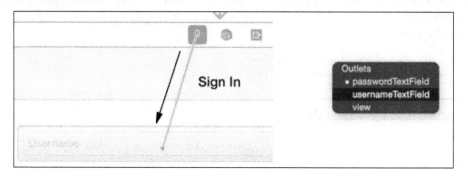

Implementing the target action pattern to launch the `signIn` method requires a very similar sequence: the `signIn` method has to be prefixed with the `@IBAction` keyword to expose it to Interface Builder. Take a look at this code:

```
@IBAction func signIn(sender:UIButton){
```

Now, again, simply press *Ctrl* and drag and drop from the **Sign In** button to the view controller icon and, as soon as you release the mouse button, you will be asked to select which method you want to connect to the `touchUpInside` event of the button.

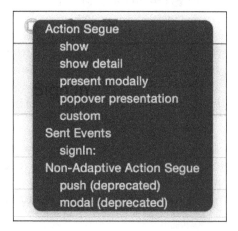

After the user sign in is completed, you probably want to present a new view controller to the authenticated user. If this controller is designed into a Storyboard, you can *instantiate it programmatically* just by referring to its *Storyboard ID*. This task is accomplished by first obtaining an instance of the Storyboard that you can use inside your code using the `init(name:Bundle:)` initializer of the `UIStoryboard` class. Run the following line of code:

```
var storyboard = UIStoryboard(name: "Main", bundle: nil)
```

This function is straightforward: it requires the name of the Storyboard and the bundle it belongs to initialize. (If the Storyboard is in the main bundle, you can just pass `nil`).

Once an instance of the Storyboard is available within the code, it can be used to instantiate the desired view controller, but a *Storyboard ID* for this controller has to be defined in the **Identity** inspector:

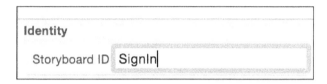

Then, the view controller can be easily initialized through the next code:

```
let welcomeVC = storyboard.instantiateViewControllerWithIdentifier
    ("Welcome") as! WelcomeViewController
```

You can also create an instance of the *initial view controller* using the `initializeInitialViewController` function.

Implementing navigation with Storyboard and segues

The whole navigation of the application can be defined using Storyboards with the help of *segues*.

A segue is an instance of the `UIStoryboardSegue` class that is normally initialized directly through a Storyboard. Its main role is to define a relationship or transition between view controllers. There are essentially two kind of segues: a *relationship segue*, which is adopted with `UINavigationViewController`, `UITabBarController`, and `UISplitViewController` to define their children view controllers, and an *adaptive segue*, which is used to transition from one view controller to another.

Creating a segue is extremely simple. Let's say you want to define the relationship between a navigation view controller and its root view controller. You can press *Ctrl* and drag from the navigation view controller to the view controller you want to set as root.

The HUD that appears when you release the mouse button allows you to set the view controllers' relationship *selecting* — in this case, "root view controller". A line with a special icon will identify that the relationship has just been created:

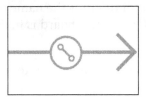

With the exact same process, you can create adaptive segues. You just need to insert a button into a view controller, press *Ctrl* and drag from this button to another controller, and select one of the possible adaptive segues presented by the gray HUD.

An adaptive segue is defined by a string *identifier*, a *source view controller* that is the segue's starting point, and a *destination view controller* that is the controller the segue will present.

There are several types of segues you can choose from, each defining how the destination view controller will be inserted into the current application structure. Take a look at the following table:

Show	This segue adds the destination view controller to the stack. Depending on the structure of the application, the new controller can be pushed into the stack or presented as a modal dialog.
Show detail	This is similar to the Show segue but more specific; if the application displays a detail master view, the destination controller replaces the detail view.
Present modally	This presents the destination view modally.
Present as a popover	When run on an iPad, this segue presents the destination controller in a popover, while on an iPhone, it is presented modally.
Custom	This presents your own custom-built segues.

You can gain full control over the segue execution overriding some `UIViewController` methods. The `shouldPerformSegueWithIdentifier(identifier:sender:)` can be implemented to define whether the segue for a given identifier has to start, while, overriding the `prepareForSegue(segue:sender:)` methods, you then have the chance to set useful information for the view controllers before the segue starts.

A really common task is to use this function to set information for the controller that will be shown. From the segue instance, you can access the `identifier` segue and the `sourceViewController` and `destinationViewController` properties to get references to the view controllers involved with the segue. Now, execute the following script:

```
override func prepareForSegue(segue: UIStoryboardSegue,
                              sender: AnyObject?) {

    if segue.identifier == "userDetails"{
        let detailsVC = segue.destinationViewController as!
                        detailsViewController
        detailsVC.firstname = user.firstname
        detailsVC.lastname = user.lastname
    }
}
```

The unwind segue

With an adaptive segue, you can set up a "one-way" navigation flow. This is obviously not enough and with *unwind segues*; the navigation flow can be reversed, moving back to a view controller previously inserted in the navigation stack. An unwind segue implementation starts from a function with a predefined prototype, as shown in the following snippet:

```
@IBAction func <function name>(segue:UIStoryboardSegue){}
```

You can add code inside this function, but to make unwind work, it is enough to define a function with this signature inside the destination view controller.

This acts *similarly to an anchor* to the view controller where the function is defined, and it is triggered by another view controller currently visible to the user. As soon as this function is triggered, the navigation stack is reorganized to show the view controller that contains the unwind function.

To set how the unwind segue can be triggered and from where, you need to link an action to the **Exit** proxy, which is the orange icon that you can find above any view controller in the interface editor:

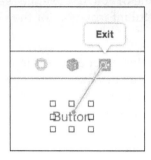

If you feel that it's a bit counterintuitive at first, don't worry; it's normal. You are, in fact, connecting the button action to a function (the unwind function), which is not in the same view controller of the button.

Hands-on code

In this exercise, you will implement a typical **Sign In / Registration Completed** navigation using only the Storyboard. Here is an image that describes the full navigation:

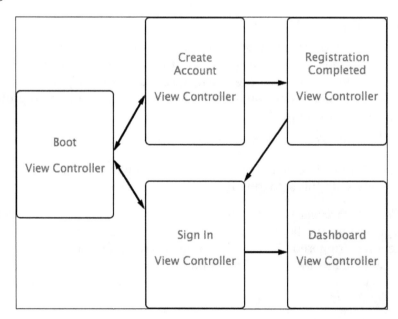

Open the `Start` project for this chapter, and you will find a complete structure of view controllers that are not connected to each other yet. While you're at it, also check the `Completed` project so that you can have a preview of the final result and verify your implementation. In the following paragraphs, we will set up the segues that implement the navigation introduced in the previous image.

The *Boot* view controller is the *initial view controller* of the Storyboard, and it is where the user can choose to sign in or create a new account. Through two adaptive segues of the *Show* type, you can connect the **Sign In** and **Create Account** buttons to the appropriate view controllers. It's really easy: just press *Ctrl* and drag from the buttons to the view controller that you want to show, and select the Show segue. At this point, you can already launch the application to check the result.

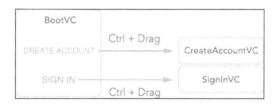

The *create account* view controller is presented through a navigation controller. From this point, the user can choose to complete the registration or go back to the boot view controller. In order to implement the complete registration section, you have to *connect* the *Done* navigation item to the next view controller. Again, you can test the full navigation by launching the application.

We can now *add some logics* to this part of the navigation. Let's say that the user has to fill at least the *username* and *password* text fields to complete the registration. Then, let's implement the `shouldPerformSegueWithIdentifier` function for `CreateAccountViewController`. Before writing any code, we need to specify an identifier for the segue. *Select* the segue you just created and set its identifier with the `completeRegistration` string. Now we can implement the function with this code:

```
override func shouldPerformSegueWithIdentifier(
                                identifier: String?,
                                  sender: AnyObject?) ->
                                    Bool {
        if identifier == "completeRegistration"{
```

```
        if usernameTextField.text != "" && passwordTextField != ""
        {
            return true
        }else{
            return false
        }
    }else{
        return true
    }
}
```

This first checks the identifier of the segue and then it allows its execution only if the username and password text fields are filled in.

The unwind segue inside the boot view controller enables the user to go back to the boot view controller. Just write the method without any code in it for now, as follows:

```
@IBAction func unwindToBoot(segue:UIStoryboardSegue){}
```

You can now *connect* the "X" left navigation item from the create account view controller to the **Exit** proxy, and the unwindToBoot segue appears as the only choice.

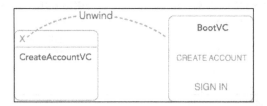

While we're here, it would be nice to have a link from the **Registration Completed** view controller straight to the sign in view controller. From the Registration Completed view controller, *connect* the **Sign In** button to the Sign In view controller with a Show segue. It's that simple!

You can now complete the Sign In navigation as a further exercise as it's extremely similar to the navigation you just implemented. Here are a couple of tips:

- Verify that the user has filled username and password text fields
- Use the prepareForSegue function to pass information to dashboardViewController
- Implement the logout using the unwindToBoot segue
- Remember that you can verify the final result using the Complete project that you find in the source code for this chapter

Summary

With this chapter, you learned how to create user interfaces with Interface Builder and how to achieve nontrivial navigation with segues. You can now experiment by mixing the information from *Chapter 2, UI Components Overview – UIKit*, and *Chapter 3, Interface Builder, XIB, and Storyboard*, to achieve more complex UIs!

With the next chapter, you will learn how to define the position and size of user interface elements in a dynamic way using *Auto Layout*.

4
Auto Layout

Before Xcode 5, Auto Layout was probably the most annoying feature you could decide to implement in your app. Flagging "Use Auto Layout" was as scary as jumping into a lion's cage, and people tended to use it with a sort of reverential fear, originating from stories told by fellow developers.

Luckily, it has improved immensely, and now, it's a completely different story: working with Auto Layout is extremely simple, and Xcode fully supports all of its features.

I would go as far as to say that Auto Layout now classifies as mandatory knowledge if you're serious about building modern user interfaces. New additions to iOS 9, such as `UIStackView`, and the growing lists of screens sizes are probably just what you need to leave all the doubts behind and start using it right away.

How Auto Layout works

With Auto Layout, you can arrange your app's UI by defining *relations* between UI elements. These relations are called **constraints**. A constraint can be defined between two different elements to set a distance between them, for instance, or it can be associated to a single element and used to define its width/height.

At first, this might sound strange, because in *Chapter 1*, *UI Fundamentals*, and *Chapter 3*, *Interface Builder, XIB, and Storyboard*, we talked about how to place subviews independently by only taking care of where to draw them and modifying their frame/bounds properties. There's more to it, however.

You can set up Auto Layout in three main ways:

- You can add all the constraints from Interface Builder directly thanks to a (almost) complete list of instruments

- You can add constraints using code thanks to **Visual Format Language** (VFL) if you need more control

- You can generate constraints automatically starting from the current autoresizing mask and `translatesAutoresizingMaskIntoConstraints;` however, we will not take this method into account in the book—let's consider it deprecated

During the rest of the chapter, I will guide you through a list of examples that will help you learn how to use Auto Layout effectively. You can consider this entire chapter as a big *hands-on code* section, and obviously, you will find the `Chapter 4` project in the book's source code.

Xcode and Auto Layout

Xcode's UI is updated to fully support Auto Layout and simplify the way we work with it. Our journey wouldn't be complete without a proper overview of the instruments we have at our disposal.

From Interface Builder, you can easily set up your constraints and Auto Layout settings. In the lower-right corner of the interface editor, you can see a bunch of icons that group different options for Auto Layout: the **Stack**, **Pin**, **Align**, and **Resolve Issue** panels. We'll talk about some of these buttons in the examples; for now, just remember that all these icons are related to Auto Layout:

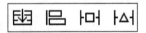

The first way to interact with Auto Layout is directly through the views. From the interface editor, put a `UIView` in a view controller's view while pressing *Ctrl* and dragging the mouse around. You will see a blue selector similar to the one you see while connecting `@IBOutlet` and `@IBaction`. In this case, if you release it over the new view, you'll see some new choices that identify Auto Layout constraints.

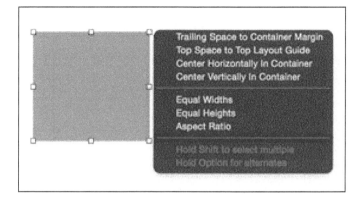

Adding a constraint to a view is extremely simple. Let's start by creating a constraint that works on a single view and doesn't have any relation with other views. Perform the following steps:

1. Press *Ctrl* and click over the view.

2. Drag the mouse while keeping a horizontal trajectory. This ensures that the **Width** parameter shows up when you release the mouse button over the same view. You can try to move vertically to obtain the height parameter.

3. Choose the **Width** parameter.

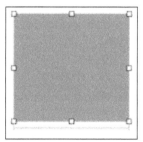

You've now created a constraint that says, *This view has a width of N points*, where *N* is the value that is currently assigned to the view via the interface editor. Disregard the red/orange line that is drawn below the view for now; we just need the width constraint to discover some other Xcode features.

If you select the view and open the **Size** inspector panel, you will find a new area called **Constraints** that contains the width constraint that you just added.

From here, you can modify or delete the added constraints.

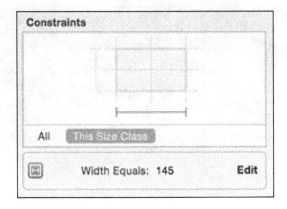

Another place where you can find information about your constraints is the *document outline*, which is the left-hand side column of the Storyboard.

As you can note, we have full access to our newly created constraint. Click on it, and it will be highlighted in the interface editor:

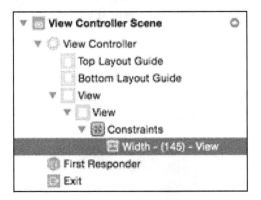

Another piece of useful information we can obtain from the document outline is the presence of Auto Layout inconsistencies or errors. The red circle with the white arrow in the upper-right corner tells us that something isn't set correctly. Now, perform the following steps:

1. Click on the arrow, and a new view will show the errors with additional details.

2. Just click on the first red dot. Xcode is smart enough to suggest you the right Auto Layout configuration.

3. Click on **Add Missing Constraints**; the needed constraints will be added to the view automatically, and all the errors will disappear.

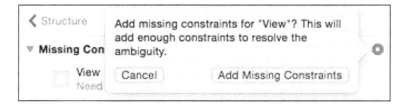

4. If you check the view from the interface editor now, you'll see the new added constraints; this time they will all be *blue*. This means that all the needed constraints are defined, and Auto Layout knows exactly how to draw your view.

Practical introduction to constraints

Now that you know how to interact with Xcode to manage constraints, we can practice with Auto Layout! A constraint is an instance of the NSLayoutConstraint class, and through Interface Builder, you can manage constraint instantiation without writing a single line of code.

The main rule we should keep in mind is that if you want to specify the frame of a view with Auto Layout, *you need to give it enough information for both the X/Y position and width/height size.* This is the first step to make it work the way it's supposed to.

Let's move to another example where you will play directly with constraints.

Open the start project for this chapter and check the controller called Example A in the Main Storyboard. You can easily move through examples using the document outline window, where all the example scenes for this chapter are listed from Example A to Example E.

The goal that we want to achieve with Example A is to create a UIView instance that is centered vertically and horizontally, regardless of screen size and orientation.

Looking at the current view controller, you can see an orange `UIView` instance that is a subview of the main view. Its size is 150 x 150, and it is placed at the center of the main view. Now that this view is placed in its desired position, you can add constraints to specify how it should behave.

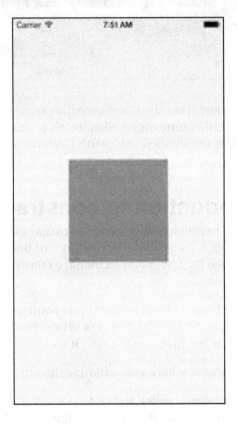

 This is a really common approach with Auto Layout: define the view size and position before adding any constraint. You don't need to care about constraints as you haven't done this initial setup yet.

Now, let's add the *size constraints* using two different methods:

- Just as you did in the previous section, press *Ctrl* and click on the new view and drag the mouse horizontally to add the *width* constraint.

- To add the height constraint, you can use the icons in the lower-right corner of the interface editor. Select the orange `UIView` instance, click on the second icon from the right, flag the **Height** parameter, and click on the **Add Constraints** button. This is an alternative way to set up a constraint.

Great! You just set all the *size constraints* for a view.

This doesn't mean that the constraints are already fully defined, though. In fact, you should notice a red circle in the document outline for `Example A` and click on it to get information about the current issues for the view. We saw that we need to set width/height and X/Y to be compliant with Auto Layout's required conditions, and Xcode helps us by highlighting what is currently missing.

We can ask Xcode to automatically adjust the errors as we did before using the **Add Missing Constraints** button, or we can manually add the needed constraints. Let's do it manually this time to take a look at how to create a relation between a *view* and its *superview*:

1. Press *Ctrl* and drag from the `UIView` instance to its superview while maintaining a vertical trajectory, as in the following figure:

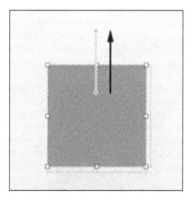

2. Release the mouse button and select **Horizontally in Container**. You can verify the new constraints in the **Size** inspector named **Align Center X to: Superview**.

3. To add the vertical (Y) information, you can use the second icon from the left in the lower-right corner of the interface editor. This panel shows the alignment constraints option. Click on the button and check the **Vertically in Container** flag. Finally, click on the **Add 1 Constraint** button to confirm:

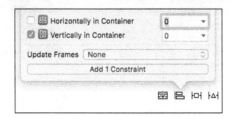

You should see two new blue lines crossing the view indicating that all the needed constraints are now in place.

4. Launch the app and switch between portrait and landscape to appreciate the final result, which is that the view is centered on the screen, regardless of the orientation. You can verify the difference in behavior by removing the constraints. In landscape mode, the view will just move out of the screen.

Xcode helpers

Another interesting feature is Xcode's ability to reset frames and constraints on the fly to automatically maintain your Auto Layout setup.

With all the previous constraints set, move the orange view to a new position (meaning change the coordinates through **Size** Inspector or just drag and drop the view without modifying the constraints).

You should see something similar to this:

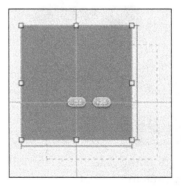

Your position constraints turn to orange, indicating the view is misplaced. A red dashed square highlights the "expected" frame, and two labels reveal the gap between this frame and the current one.

You have a lot of information shown in the document outline. This time, the indicator is not red but yellow to indicate the wrong placement more as a warning than an error. Indeed, the *Auto Layout conditions are still valid*, even though what you are seeing in the Storyboard is not the runtime result. If you click on the yellow dot, Xcode will provide more useful information about the view position, indicating the actual and the expected values:

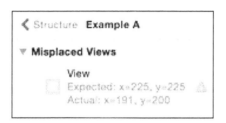

How can you solve this situation? First, you have to decide what your desired result is:

- Do you want to keep the initial setup? If this is the case, click on the fourth icon in the lower-right corner of the interface editor (the one with the triangle at the center) and select **Update Frames**. The view will just move to reflect the runtime frame (the red dotted one), which is defined by constraints.

- Do you want to update the runtime frame? Click again on the icon and select **Update Constraints** to *change the constraints* to match the current frame:

Try them both so that you can see the difference between the two.

Intrinsic content size

Let's move on to the Example B view controller. In this example, we will obtain the exact same result of Example A (a vertically and horizontally centered view) using UILabel instead of UIView.

Move to Example B, simply add the *position constraints* for the label, and you are done! You don't need to set up any size constraint. Take a look at the result by launching the app. The label is exactly at the center of the window:

You can obtain this result because some leaf objects, such as buttons and labels, define their size depending on their content. The intrinsicContentSize method of UIView (and inherited by all subclasses) is responsible for returning the desired size, so you shouldn't overload this information with constraints. The intrinsic content size is calculated by the view itself and used by Auto Layout to create the constraints to define the size of an element. These constraints can be overridden by "normal" constraints, such as the ones you previously added.

Constraints, for a view that defines its intrinsic content size, can be defined even more through the *content hugging priority* and *content compression resistance* properties. They work in conjunction with another NSLayoutConstraint property, priority. Constraints with a higher priority are satisfied before constraints with lower priority.

The hugging and compression properties define in which order Auto Layout should calculate the size of a view that uses intrinsic content size. For example, you can define a label width just using two constraints that link the right- and left-hand sides of the label to the left- and right-hand side of the label's superview. Depending on the value you assign to these constraints and on the size of the superview, the label width changes dynamically.

Since the label has an intrinsic content size value that is automatically generated depending on the content of the label text, you can use hugging and compression resistance to force the label size to maintain its intrinsic content size. By default, the priority value of the trail and lead constraints defined in the previous image is equal to UILayoutPriorityRequired, which in turn is equal to 1000.

To prevent the label from growing independently from the label's intrinsic size, you have to set a hugging priority that is higher than the priority of the trail and lead constraints. This means that if you set the constraints priority to UILayoutPriorityLow (250) and the hugging priority to 1000, the intrinsic content size takes precedence in the width calculation process. This will be the final result:

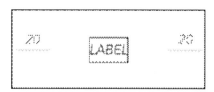

Compression resistance works in a really similar way: instead of forcing the size of the element not to grow, it ensures that the content size is not reduced to values lower than the initial intrinsic size. Let's take a look at the images; the one on the left-hand side shows how the label will be sized if you don't set compression resistance, while the image on the right-hand side illustrates how compression resistance forces the label width to a minimum needed size:

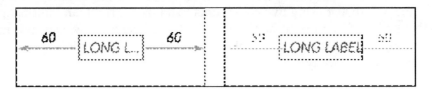

Independence from screen size

When you need to create a user interface that works on different screen sizes or simply in both the portrait and landscape orientations, Auto Layout can make a real difference.

Let's switch to `Example C`. What you see here is a really common situation: we need to create a layout that works for any screen size and orientation. These images are a preview of the final result:

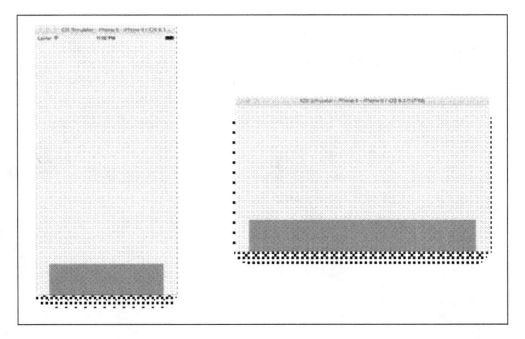

The *footer* view of this example has two defining characteristics that you have to take into account:

- Its width changes depending on the screen size
- It is attached to the bottom of the screen

Remember the procedure we discussed; we have to satisfy both position and size constraints and then add the needed constraints to achieve the desired result.

We can use a particular reference helper to attach the view to the bottom of the screen: the *bottom layout guide*. This element indicates the lowest visible point of the main view, and it can be linked directly through Interface Builder. It is displayed in the document outline as the first child of the view controller, and it is also available at the bottom of the main view in the interface editor.

You can just press *Ctrl* and drag from the footer view to the bottom layout guide and then select **Vertical Spacing** to specify that you want to keep the footer view at a fixed distance from the bottom. You can create new constraints from the document outline, as illustrated in the following image:

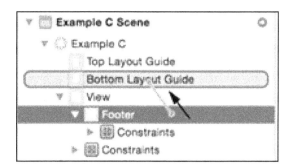

You can set the width of the footer dynamically by defining the distance between its left- and right-hand sides and the screen's left-hand and right-hand side margins. These two relations automatically cause the width of the view to change when the superview size changes.

To create these relations, just press *Ctrl* and drag from the footer view to the left-hand side of the screen and select **Leading Space to Container Margin**, and then press *Ctrl* and drag to the right-hand side and select **Trailing Space to Container Margin**.

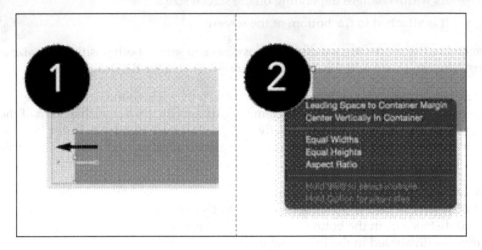

Well done! We have now satisfied all the size constraints. The bottom of the footer view is attached to the bottom of the main view, and its width dynamically changes depending on the screen's orientation and size.

> Margins can be used to create internal padding for any view. The margin value is defined by layoutMargins, a UIEdgeInsets instance that comes with a value of eight for the top, bottom, left, and right margins by default. When you define a constraint to the side of a view that has a margin, this margin is added to the constraint's constant value.

Updating constraints programmatically

At times, if you want to obtain a complex positioning of your views, you need a little more control over constraints. Constraints are just instances of the NSLayoutConstraint class; therefore, we can access some of its properties at runtime programmatically.

Moving to `Example D`, you'll see a dark orange view attached to the bottom of the screen (let's call it *footer view*):

That view covers more than 50% of the screen while in portrait. Without any update on the constraints, when we change the orientation to landscape, the layout results in something totally different from the portrait layout, with the footer view covering the whole screen.

In this example, some constraints are already added to the view; the footer view has a fixed height and a width equal to the main view and is horizontally centered inside the main view. The `Example D` controller is associated with the `ResizerViewController` class, a custom class where you can write the code for this example.

The result we are looking for is:

- Resizing programmatically the footer view, depending on screen orientation
- Obtaining a layout that can show both the main and the footer views, even in the landscape orientation

A quick way to reach this goal consists in updating the height constraint at runtime as soon as the device orientation changes. The constraints can be referenced from your code exactly as you do with a UI component by just prefixing a property with the @IBOutlet keyword, as follows:

```
@IBOutlet var CST_Height:NSLayoutConstraint!
```

Then, you can just link the property using Interface Builder. In the document outline, you should easily find the right constraint:

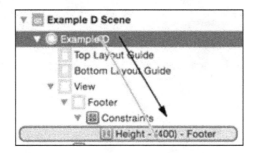

The new value will be associated to the constant property of the constraint. Execute the following code:

```
override func willAnimateRotationToInterfaceOrientation(
    toInterfaceOrientation: UIInterfaceOrientation,
    duration: NSTimeInterval) {

        if UIInterfaceOrientationIsLandscape
          (toInterfaceOrientation){
            CST_Height.constant = heightForLandscape
        }else{
            CST_Height.constant = heightForPortrait
        }
        footerView.setNeedsUpdateConstraints()
}
```

The willAnimateRotationToInterfaceOrientation function is automatically called every time the orientation changes. From the preceding code, you can note that we set a new value for the constant property depending on the new orientation, which in turn is evaluated through the UIInterfaceOrientationIsLandscape function (in the next chapter, you'll learn how to use *trait classes* instead of referring to interface orientations).

In the last line, the setNeedsUpdateConstraints function is called on a reference of the footer view. This function ensures that the constraints for this view are updated as soon as possible by the system through the updateConstraints function.

Note that you can achieve this goal by also defining the relationships of views, such as "Keep the footer view's height always equal to the half of the parent view's height". You'll learn how to work with views relationship in the next pages.

Working with Auto Layout programmatically

An interesting way to interact with Auto Layout is through the VFL, a simple language introduced by Apple to handle constraints at runtime.

With VFL, you can define constraints using a simple syntax. You can define the width and height of an element using these strings, for example:

```
"H:[element(100)]"
```

```
"V:[element(100)]"
```

The first uppercase character tells which dimension you want to modify. *H* stands for horizontal and *V* for vertical. The rest of the string defines the details of the constraints.

Initializing the views

Let's move to Example E to write our first VFL code.

The layout for this example is based on two simple UIView instances that you can add to the main view of the controller via code. In the next pages, you will modify these views by applying constraints via VFL only. All the code you see here is available in the VFLViewController.swift file.

The first step is initializing all the views using the viewDidLoad function. Let's call the two new views — redView and greenView — by executing the following code:

```
override func viewDidLoad() {
    super.viewDidLoad()

    redView.setTranslatesAutoresizingMaskIntoConstraints(false)
    redView.backgroundColor = UIColor.redColor()

    greenView.setTranslatesAutoresizingMaskIntoConstraints(false)
    greenView.backgroundColor = UIColor.greenColor()

    view.addSubview(redView)
    view.addSubview(greenView)
}
```

When you have to deal with Auto Layout programmatically, it is good practice to turn `translatesAutoresizingMaskIntoConstraints` off. This ensures that no constraint is created automatically for the views eliminating the risk of it conflicting with auto-resizing constraints (when you add constraints from IB, it automatically sets this property to `false`).

Adding constraints

When working with Auto Layout programmatically, you essentially have to complete these three steps:

1. Define the element involved in the VFL definition.

2. Write the VFL definition.

3. Attach the constraints to the correct view.

To satisfy step 1, we can use the computed properties and generate a dictionary via the following script:

```
var viewsDictionary: [NSObject:AnyObject] {
    get {
        return ["redView":self.redView,
                "greenView":self.greenView]
    }
}
```

Step 2 requires VFL definitions. Let's say that for this first example, we want to draw a red square and place it at a fixed distance from the upper-left corner of the main view.

We already know how to define the size through VFL; simply run the following:

```
"H:[redView(100)]"
```

```
"V:[redView(100)]"
```

We can then set the `redView` view's position in a similar way. With the next definitions, we want to create constraints to set the distance of the view from the upper and left-hand side of the main view. We can do this as follows:

```
"H:|-20-[redView]"
```

```
"V:|-20-[redView]"
```

Again, *H* defines the horizontal information, while *V* defines the vertical information. It may help if we translate the first VFL string in a simple sentence. The `"H:|-20-[redView]"` part of the code stands for *red view must maintain a distance of 20 points from the left-hand side of its superview.*

By writing the string as `"H:[redView]-20-|"`, we say that the distance has to be calculated from the right-hand side of the superview instead.

The pipe character (|) can be read as a reference to the *superview* of the object between square brackets.

The same applies for the *vertical* orientation. This time, a pipe on the left-hand side means *top* (side or margin), while on the right, it means *bottom*.

As we discussed previously, constraints are defined by the `NSLayoutConstraint` class. You can attach new constraints to a view with the `UIView` instance's `addConstraint(s):` method and remove them with `removeConstraint(s):`. We can complete step 3 using these functions.

Here's the code that we need to generate the constraints mentioned before:

```
// Set Size
let cst_height = NSLayoutConstraint.constraintsWithVisualFormat(
                    "V:[redView(100)]",
                    options: NSLayoutFormatOptions.allZeros,
                    metrics: nil,
                    views: viewsDictionary)
let cst_width = NSLayoutConstraint.constraintsWithVisualFormat(
                    "H:[redView(100)]",
                    options: NSLayoutFormatOptions.allZeros,
                    metrics: nil,
                    views: viewsDictionary)


// Set Position
let cst_Y = NSLayoutConstraint.constraintsWithVisualFormat(
                    "V:|-30-[redView]",
                    options: NSLayoutFormatOptions.allZeros,
                    metrics: nil,
                    views: viewsDictionary)
let cst_X = NSLayoutConstraint.constraintsWithVisualFormat(
                    "H:|-20-[redView]",
                    options: NSLayoutFormatOptions.allZeros,
                    metrics: nil,
                    views: viewsDictionary)
```

This is a lot of code, but as you can see, it is extremely simple. You can generate an array of constraints through the `constraintsWithVisualFormat` function by passing the VFL string as the first parameter and the dictionary of views involved in the VFL as the last one. The keys defined within the dictionary are really important because they are used with the VFL strings to refer to the appropriate objects.

Now that we have defined the constraints, it's time to add them to the views using the `addConstraints:` method:

```
self.redView.addConstraints(cst_height)
self.redView.addConstraints(cst_width)

self.view.addConstraints(cst_Y)
self.view.addConstraints(cst_X)
```

The constraints related to the size of the view are attached to `redView` directly. The view receiving the constraints related to the `redView` view's position is the main view, though. Keep this in mind: it is the parent view's responsibility to assign the proper position to its children. In our case, the main view receives the constraints to properly position `redView` within its bounds.

The final result is in the following image:

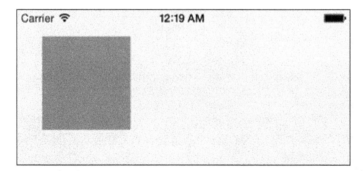

Working with multiple views

In the next example, we will include the green view in the app layout. The `greenView` view should be placed next to `redView` using only VFL, again. Here is the final result:

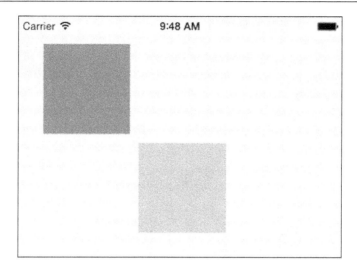

The definition of the greenView view's size is identical to what we previously saw with redView, so let's focus on the code needed to define the greenView view's position:

```
// Set Position
let cst_Y = NSLayoutConstraint.constraintsWithVisualFormat(
    "V:[redView]-10-[greenView]",
    options: NSLayoutFormatOptions.allZeros,
    metrics: nil,
    views: viewsDictionary)
let cst_X = NSLayoutConstraint.constraintsWithVisualFormat(
    "H:[redView]-10-[greenView]",
    options: NSLayoutFormatOptions.allZeros,
    metrics: nil,
    views: viewsDictionary)
```

The VFL definitions simply add constraints between the right-hand side of redView and the left-hand side of greenView ("H:[redView]-10-[greenView]") and from the bottom of redView to the top of greenView ("V:[redView]-10-[greenView]").

Remember that the constraintsWithVisualFormat function returns an array of constraints. This means that we could even define the constraints for redView and greenView in the same definition with these VFL strings:

```
"H:|-20-[redView]-10-[greenView]"
"V:|-20-[redView]-10-[greenView]"
```

Relations between views

Another really cool Auto Layout feature is the ability to edit an attribute of a view in relation to an attribute from another view. With this kind of interaction, you can achieve really complex behaviors.

The function that lets you easily create these relations is the `init(item:attri bute:relatedBy:toItem:attribute:multiplier:constant:)` initializer of `NSLayoutConstraint`.

Thanks to this initializer, you can create constraints such as *the greenView view's height has to be half that of the redView view's width plus 10 points*. Here is the necessary code:

```
let cst_height = NSLayoutConstraint(
    item: greenView,
    attribute: NSLayoutAttribute.Height,
    relatedBy: NSLayoutRelation.Equal,
    toItem: redView,
    attribute: NSLayoutAttribute.Height,
    multiplier: 0.5,
    constant: 10.0)
```

This uses an equality relation (`NSLayoutRelation.Equal`) to associate a value to the `greenView` view's width (`NSLayoutAttribute.Width`), starting from the `redView` view's width multiplied by the multiplier (`0.5`) and adding a constant value (`10.0`).

We can easily convert this sentence to an expression that's way more readable, as follows:

```
greenView.height = redView.width * 0.5 + 10.0
```

Keep in mind that this constraint has to be attached to the *main view* and not to `greenView`. This might sound a bit counterintuitive as in the previous examples, you learned that size constraints should be attached directly to the interested object. With relationships, you are working with more than one view, though; therefore, the main logic is quite different.

Another difference with the previous example consists in the fact that we won't receive an array of constraints but just a single constraint. This means that we have to use the `addConstraint` function instead of `addConstraints`, as follows:

```
self.view.addConstraint(cst_height)
```

This will be the final result:

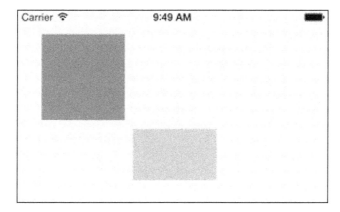

Summary

In this chapter, we covered all the basics of Auto Layout, and you learned how you can create dynamic user interfaces that easily adapt to different screen sizes and orientations.

With the next chapter, we'll expand on these basics and move on to create fully adaptive user interfaces.

5
Adaptive User Interfaces

Before iOS 8, if we wanted to define how to display content, we had to perform checks on the screen size of our device on the current orientation or on the device model. These techniques have been good friends of ours in the past, but with an ever-growing number of screens sizes to take into account, this information is no longer enough. We need a more dynamic way to refer to screen sizes and formats.

In this chapter, you will learn how Apple has improved the way you can conceive and build adaptive user interfaces through some brand new and welcome additions to Cocoa Touch, such as *size classes*, *trait environments*, and *UIStackViews*.

UI definition with size classes

When working with iOS applications, you used to think about a device screen in terms of size, orientation, and device type. Now forget about it! We will start from scratch and take a look at how to create *adaptive layouts* using *size classes*.

Conceptually, a size class is extremely simple. It is a way to express vertical and horizontal sizes through only two possible values: *regular* or *compact*. As the two words imply, you can define that an object size (vertical or horizontal) is just at its regular (read "big") or compact (also, "small") format.

As you can note with these two definitions, we are not saying anything about orientation or device; we just say that a generic object has, for example, *a vertical compact size* and a *horizontal regular size*. This generic object interface can be defined to behave differently, depending on its size classes—not on the device type, orientation, or specific size.

The `UIUserInterfaceSizeClass` enum defines a size class. Here is its full declaration:

```
enum UIUserInterfaceSizeClass : Int {
    case Unspecified
```

```
    case Compact
    case Regular
}
```

All the possible combinations of size classes are described by this matrix:

What takes a bit getting used to is the way Apple devices are inserted inside this matrix. Here's a list of all the combinations of devices and orientations and how they fit the matrix:

	Regular (horizontal)	Compact (horizontal)
Regular (vertical)	• iPad (landscape) • iPad (portrait)	• iPhone 6 Plus (portrait) • iPhone 6, 5, 4 (portrait)
Compact (vertical)	iPhone 6 Plus (landscape)	iPhone 6, 5, 4 (landscape)

The first time you look at this grid, you might get confused by the way iPad is categorized. You don't have a way to distinguish between landscape and portrait as in both orientations, the size classes are identical.

Whether this feels right or not, it's something you have to live with; however, don't worry, you can always rely on a new function that is added to the `UIViewController` class starting from iOS 8: `viewWillTransitionToSize:coordinator:`. This function gives you the size of the device every time it is about to be updated. Even if Apple suggests working mostly with size classes, if you really need to perform specific operations related to the screen orientation, you might want to override this function in your controllers. Another really common way to intercept the device's orientation is to work with the `UIDevice` class, which posts the `UIDeviceOrientationDidChange` notification and has some useful properties, such as `orientation`, and methods, such as `UIDeviceOrientationIsLandscape:/Portrait:`.

A size class is used in conjunction with a *trait*, a new concept added from iOS 8 onward to specify the nature of the adaptive user interface.

User interface's traits

A trait consists of a set of properties that determines how the user interface or a portion of it should change as its environment or, more broadly, the available space for its contents and changes.

These properties include size classes for both horizontal and vertical dimensions as well as display scale, user interface idiom, and `forceTouchCapability`, and they define a *trait collection*.

Trait collection and trait environment

Designing adaptive user interfaces essentially means writing layouts that adapt according to changes in trait collections.

The `UITraitCollection` class is the data type that defines a trait collection and it is the entry point for the traits we described earlier. The following table illustrates the properties that are part of a trait collection:

Trait	Description
• `verticalSizeClass` • `(UIUserInterfaceSizeClass)`	This is the vertical size class for the trait collection; the possible values for this property are `.Regular`, `.Compact`, or `.Unspecified`.
• `horizontalSizeClass` • `(UIUserInterfaceSizeClass)`	This is the horizontal size class for the trait collection; the possible values for this property are `.Regular`, `.Compact`, or `.Unspecified`.

Trait	Description
• `userInterfaceIdiom` • (`UIUserInterfaceIdiom`)	This defines the idiom of the user interface; the possible values are `.Phone`, `.Pad`, and `.Unspecified`.
• `displayScale` • (`CGFloat`)	This is the scale adopted by the screen; for a retina display, this value is `2.0`, while for the iPhone 6 Plus, it is `3.0`. It is `1.0` for other older devices such as iPhone 3G or for the first model of iPad Mini.
• `forceTouchCapability` • (`UIForceTouchCapability`)	The force touch is a new feature available on iPhone 6s and 6s Plus. The possible values for this property are `.Available`, `.Unavailable`, and `.Unknown`.

A trait collection is strictly related to the *trait environment protocol*, (`UITraitEnvironment`) to which some important classes, such as `UIScreen`, `UIWindow`, `UIViewControllers`, and `UIView`, conform. All these classes, as they implement this protocol, can return a trait collection through the `traitCollection` property. This property describes the current trait collection they are adopting.

A trait environment is defined starting from the screen, and it is then passed down through the entire hierarchy reaching the leaf views. This means that, by default, a UI element inherits the trait collection from its parent.

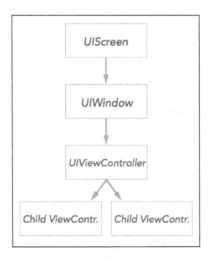

A class implementing the `UITraitEnvironment` protocol can be informed about any change on the current trait collection through the `traitCollectionDidChange:` method. This method is called as soon as a property of the trait collection changes. You can update your UI in relation to the new traits after an orientation change on iPhone, for example. Another method that intercepts changes in the current traits is `willTransitionToTraitCollection(_:withTransitionCoordinator:)`.

It is called just before `traitCollectionDidChange:`, and it shares the current transition coordinator, which is useful to intercept and edit the animation that is performed during the transition (after the rotation of the iPhone screen, for instance).

 These methods are not called when a screen rotation on iPad happens as the size classes are the same.

Working with trait collections

You can initialize trait collections using the `UITraitCollection` class methods. Some of these methods create trait collections that specify values for a single trait only, leaving the other traits unspecified. Take a look at the following table:

Method	Description
`init(userInterfaceIdiom:)`	This takes `UIUserInterfaceIdiom` as an argument and specifies `userInterfaceIdiom` only
`init(displayScale:)`	This takes `CGFloat` as an argument and specifies the display scale only
`init(horizontalSizeClass:)`	This takes `UIUserInterfaceSizeClass` as an argument and specifies the horizontal size class
`init(verticalSizeClass:)`	This takes `UIUserInterfaceSizeClass` as an argument and specifies the vertical size class
`init(forceTouchCapability:)`	This takes `UIForceTouchCapability` as an argument and specifies the force touch availability

We can perform interesting operations between two different trait collections; for instance, we can check whether a trait collection is contained within another using the containsTraitsInCollection: function. This function returns true if all the Traits specified in the trait collection passed as arguments are available in the trait collection instance that called the function. Here is a simple example:

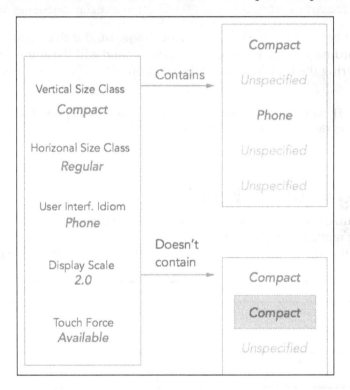

A function that takes advantage of the ability of handling multiple trait collections is the init(traitsFromCollections:) function. It receives an array of trait collections and returns a single merged element. The order of the array defines how the traits are merged; the last trait that specifies a value is taken as the value for the resulting trait collection.

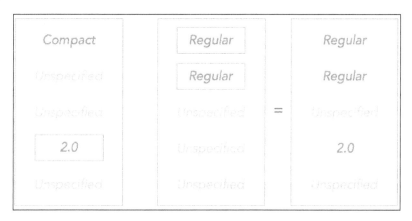

As we saw previously, a trait collection is inherited from the parent, and it cannot be updated just by setting a value for the traitCollection property (which is read-only).

The only chance we have to override this value is by injecting a view controller into the hierarchy just before the element whose trait collection we want to change and then calling the setOverrideTraitCollection(traitCollection: forChildViewController:) function. Here is a sample block of code to perform this change:

```
// Define a TraitCollection
let traits = UITraitCollection(horizontalSizeClass: .Regular)

// Add a new child into the hierarchy
let childVC = initializeChildViewController()
self.addChildViewController(childVC)
childVC.view.frame = childViewFrame

// Override the child traits
self.setOverrideTraitCollection(traits, forChildViewController:
    childVC)
self.view.addSubview(childVC.view)

childVC.didMoveToParentViewController(self)
```

Custom container view controllers are beyond the scope of this book. It suffices to say that a view controller can add other view controllers as children, creating a hierarchy of view controllers. Examples of container view controllers are `UINavigationViewController`, `UITabBarController`, and `UISplitViewController`.

Size classes and Interface Builder

Storyboard and XIB files can be used in conjunction with size classes. You can think of this as the ability to specify different layouts in the same file without adding a single line of code.

This is obviously a huge improvement to our workflow; among other things, we can now define universal applications using the same Storyboard for iPad and iPhone without duplicating all the `IBOutlet` and `IBAction` connections and subsequently update just a single file instead of keeping two different Storyboards synchronized.

Hands-on code

Let's explore this with a simple example of how easy it is to handle size classes with Interface Builder.

The main goal of the next example is creating a layout that's suitable for iPhone and another one that looks great on iPad, using the same Storyboard for both. We will create a simple hierarchy based on two views that we will call "Menu view" and "Detail view". It is something similar to what we can obtain using `UISplitViewController`, but in this case, we will work with views only, just to keep it as simple as possible.

Here's a preview of the final structure:

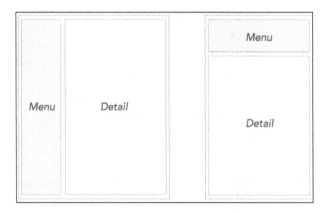

The image on the left-hand side describes the iPad layout; the **Menu** view is displayed as a fixed column to the left, and the **Detail** view gets all the remaining space. The layout works the same way in both the landscape and portrait orientations.

The image to the right is the iPhone layout; as you can see, the structure is completely different. The **Menu** view is displayed at the top of the **Detail** view, creating a sort of top bar.

Creating these layouts is extremely simple thanks to size classes. As you already learned, the size traits for iPad are *regular width* and *regular height* for both orientations, while for iPhone (let's disregard iPhone 6 Plus for this example) are *compact width* and *regular height* in portrait and *compact width* and *compact height* in landscape.

Let's start with the iPad layout first. All the magic takes place in the bottom area of Interface Builder, where you can find the size classes selector that, by default, indicates that you are working on a "generic" size class defined as w:Any h:Any.

When we define constraints for this state, we are defining constraints that are used for any size class. Just click on this area and the size class selector appears.

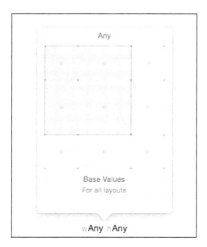

If we move the mouse cursor around over this selector, we will see that you can choose among a number of different combinations for the width/height size class. We can select all the combinations available for *regular*, *compact*, and *any* for the *width* and *height* sizes.

We chose to start from the iPad layout; let's now select the appropriate size classes for this device. To do this, starting from the selector, move your mouse to the lower-right corner until you get **Regular Width | Regular Height**. As soon as we confirm our selection by clicking on the dialog box, the lower area of Interface Builder will update the current size classes, and a blue bar will remind us that we are writing constraints for the specified traits only.

	w Regular h Regular	

We can now add some constraints required to set up the Menu view. You learned how to handle Auto Layout constraints in *Chapter 4, Auto Layout*. You can easily add the necessary constraints to the **Menu** view, as listed here (the precise name of the constraints may be slightly different, depending on the version of Xcode you're using — just keep the next constraints as general reference):

- Width = 195 (press *Ctrl* and drag horizontally over the view)
- Leading spacing to superview = 0 (press *Ctrl* and drag to the left-hand side border of the view controller)
- Vertical spacing to top layout guide = 0 (press *Ctrl* and drag to the upper border of the view controller)
- Vertical spacing to bottom layout guide = 0 (press *Ctrl* and drag to the lower border of the view controller)

With these constraints, the Menu view will be attached to the left of the screen, occupying the whole screen's height with a fixed width.

For the Detail view, create these constraints:

- Leading spacing to Menu view = 0
- Trailing spacing to superview = 0
- Vertical spacing to top layout guide = 0
- Vertical spacing to bottom layout guide = 0

Detail View's left-hand side is connected to the right-hand side of Menu View, and its height occupies the whole screen.

We can check the result by launching the app on the iPad simulator or on the device itself.

Now, let's go back to the size class selector and switch to the iPhone size classes to manage both the portrait and landscape orientations by selecting **Compact Width | Any Height** (note that starting from Xcode 7, in the class size selector, you will see "base values" instead of "Any" until you pick a selection). This combination intercepts both the regular and compact heights.

As soon as we switch to these size classes, the lower area of Interface Builder will indicate the new values. If we now look at the constraint we previously created, we can see that they are faded out.

This indicates that these constraints are not taken into consideration for these traits, but they are still available for another combination.

Another interesting piece of information is available by selecting a constraint and looking at the **Size** inspector to the right of the screen. If we select the width constraint for the Menu view, for example, we can see for which size classes it is installed (in this case, `"w:R h:R"`) and we can select/unselect the "Installed" box to install/uninstall the constraint for the current size class.

 You can also uninstall a constraint for the current size classes by selecting the constraint from the document outline and pressing *Cmd + Backspace*. If you press *Backspace* only, the constraint will be removed from all the size classes.

Let's create the constraints for the iPhone layout now. Add the following constraints for the Menu view:

- Height = 155
- Leading spacing to superview = 0

- Trailing spacing to superview = 0
- Vertical spacing to top layout guide = 0

For the Detail view, add:

- Top space to the Menu view = 0
- Leading spacing to superview = 0
- Trailing spacing to superview = 0
- Vertical spacing to bottom layout guide = 0

Done! You can now launch the application on both iPhone and iPad to see the different layouts we have chosen according to the size class.

Image assets and size classes

A similar logic can be applied to the images that we include in our projects through the xcassets folder.

When we add a new imageset, by default, we get three slots that allow us to define the 1x, 2x, and 3x image formats. These images are available for all size classes.

When we need to set a specific image for one or more size classes, it is always possible to expand the image slots list with a more granular configuration. By selecting the image from the xcassets viewer and opening the **Attributes** editor, you can find a full list of traits definable for the image. One of the things we can do is define specific slots for each device type, and we can even set slots for each combination of size traits!

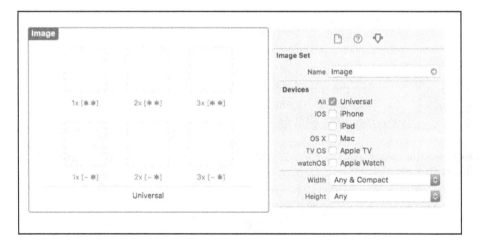

The slots available for each image will be updated depending on the configuration we set in the **Attribute** inspector. For example, if we change the width value to **Any & Regular**, we will get six slots whose names are indicated by the scale factor (1x, 2x, and 3x) and size class.

This last value is expressed through a combination of the "+", "-", and "*" characters, wrapped by square brackets, similar to [* *]. The "*" character means "Any", "+" means "Regular", and "-"" stands for "Compact". Depending on the position inside the square brackets, they identify width or height; the width is the first element, while height is the second, as with [width height].

Here are some examples to understand how to read the names of the imageset slots:

Name	Width	Height
[* *]	Any	Any
[+ *]	Regular	Any
[* -]	Any	Compact

Working with Dynamic Type

With the introduction of iOS 7, the way we work with text has greatly improved. The whole iOS structure has been refined to make it easier for us to complete complex tasks with the help of an easier-to-use framework: *Text Kit*. The main controls based on text, such as UILabel, UITextField, and UITextView are defined at the top of Text Kit.

Before iOS 7, the only way to handle text layout was working with Web views or text core, a really complex framework that is still at the base of the text drawing. Fortunately, thanks to Text Kit, you are much less likely to work directly with it now.

We won't explore Text Kit in detail here, but we will definitely talk about one of its features that is closely related to adaptive layouts: Dynamic Types.

Configurable text size

Before diving into Dynamic Types, it is important to talk about *text sizes*, a new option that iOS users can access via their device settings.

This feature has received a lot of support from Apple since its introduction in iOS 7, and it is moved from the **General** settings section to the **Display & Brightness** menu on iOS 9. This is how the view appears in iOS 9:

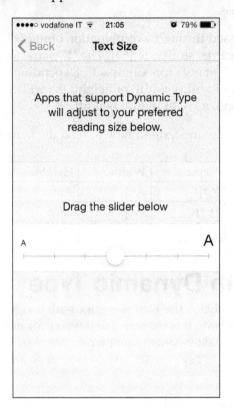

A user can essentially choose a preferred text size, depending on his/her reading preferences and, if your application is implemented using Dynamic Type, the text size of your UI elements will be adjusted accordingly.

As you can imagine, this has a lot to do with layout adaptivity. This is because your design has to change dynamically to fit user preferences.

Exploring text styles

The first step in order to understand and take advantage of Dynamic Type is to learn what a *text style* is.

You are probably used to defining fonts by setting the font size and font family. This definition is really strict, in that you are setting fixed sizes via specific numeric values.

A text style is more likely to be intended as a semantic description that doesn't give any information about font size but describes the way the font is used within the text context. Now, you can choose between six different styles with quite self-explanatory names:

- `UIFontTextStyleTitle(1,2,3)`
- `UIFontTextStyleHeadline`
- `UIFontTextStyleSubheadline`
- `UIFontTextStyleBody`
- `UIFontTextStyleCallout`
- `UIFontTextStyleFootnote`
- `UIFontTextStyleCaption1`
- `UIFontTextStyleCaption2`

Each text style, depending on the user's preferences, is associated with specific traits and a font size that is not under our control.

The simplest way to create UI elements that use text styles is through Interface Builder. We can easily select the desired style from the font panel on the **Attribute** inspector.

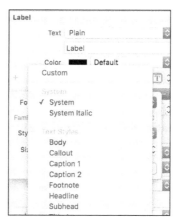

As you can see, this option overrides any previous setup, even the font family. This is one of the limitations you will encounter using Text Style; the only supported font is the system font.

To programmatically obtain a font trait that is consistent with the user's preferences, we can use the UIFont class's preferredFontForTextStyle: method. This function receives one of the text styles listed in the preceding screenshot and returns an instance of UIFont that matches the *size chosen by the user* and the traits for the required style. It is also possible to use a variant of this function provided by the UIFontDescriptor class, preferredFontDescriptorWithTextStyle:, which returns a font descriptor instead of a UIFont instance.

It is very important to note that the fonts of the UI elements are not updated automatically when the user sets a new text size from the settings. The replacement of the sizes takes place only when the view that contains these elements is reloaded.

You can improve the responsiveness of your user interfaces by intercepting these changes observing the UIContentSizeCategoryDidChangeNotification notification, thrown by the system as soon as the current preferred font size is changed.

With the user's information for this notification, you'll receive the current size category (for example, UIContentSizeCategoryExtraSmall, UIContentSizeCategoryMedium, UIContentSizeCategoryLarge, or other possible values). The same value can be retrieved at any time using the preferredContentSizeCategory property of UIApplication.

Here is an example that registers the current class as an observer of the right notification, along with a function that updates all the text elements with dynamic text:

```
override func viewDidLoad() {
    super.viewDidLoad()

    let nc = NSNotificationCenter.defaultCenter()
    nc.addObserver(self,
        selector: "updatePreferredContentSize:",
        name: UIContentSizeCategoryDidChangeNotification,
        object: nil)
}

func updatePreferredContentSize(notif: NSNotification) {

    titleLabel.font =  UIFont.preferredFontForTextStyle
        (UIFontTextStyleHeadline)

    bodyLabel.font = UIFont.preferredFontForTextStyle
        (UIFontTextStyleBody)
}
```

When adopting text styles, you are supposed to use system fonts. It is obviously possible to use our custom fonts, but Apple doesn't provide us with anything that allows us to do this automatically. At the same time, we have all the information we need to build UIFont instances, starting from the current content size category and a font style. We can implement a method that takes these two parameters and returns a font, for instance. Here is a really simple extension of the UIFont class that returns a *Dynamic* font with the *Courier* font family:

```
extension UIFont {

    static func preferredCourierForTextStyle(textStyle:String)
    ->UIFont?{

        let app = UIApplication.sharedApplication()
        let sizeCategory = app.preferredContentSizeCategory
        var fontSize:CGFloat
        var fontName:String

        // Setup Font Size
        // this example handles only some size categories...
        switch sizeCategory {
           case UIContentSizeCategoryExtraExtraExtraLarge:
            fontSize = 25.0
           case UIContentSizeCategoryMedium:
            fontSize = 20
           default:
            fontSize = 15.0
        }

        // Setup Font type
        // this example handles only some text styles...
        switch textStyle {
            case UIFontTextStyleHeadline:
            fallthrough
            case UIFontTextStyleSubheadline:
                fontName = "Courier-Bold"
            default:
                fontName = "Courier"
        }

        return UIFont(name: fontName, size: fontSize)
    }
}
```

This code builds the font instance using the information retrieved from user settings and the required text style. It is far from a complete implementation, but it is a good point to start from if you want to handle custom fonts with Dynamic Type.

Improving Auto Layout structures with UIStackView

Along with iOS 9, comes a long list of new features. The UIStackView class is one of the most interesting for sure.

Getting used to Auto Layout requires a bit of perseverance, but even when you already feel comfortable with the tool, you need to deal with the maintenance of your constraints. Depending on the complexity of the user interfaces, you might find yourself surrounded by constraints! Even if you try to keep the structure well organized, a day will come when you really need to add "those new buttons", and your well-organized structure eventually needs to be reorganized by deleting, moving, and creating new "stuff".

Thanks to UIStackView, we can dramatically simplify this structure by leveraging a system built on Auto Layout that hides most of the UI complexity by handling constraints for us automatically.

A stack view is essentially an element that's capable of displacing its subviews autonomously along a predefined axis: *vertical* or *horizontal*. We can instruct the stack view as to how subviews should be distributed just by specifying some of its internal properties. The stack view will generate and handle all the needed constraints for us, ending up in a much cleaner structure that can be easily updated and reorganized.

Setting up UIStackView

Just as for the other UIKit elements, we can create UIStackView programmatically or via Interface Builder. This time, going the IB way has some really huge advantages, including the ease of use and simplicity of setup.

With Interface Builder, we have different ways to create a stack view. We can just drag and drop the UIStackView element into a Storyboard/XIB file and drag and drop other views inside the stack view. Alternatively, we can use the **Embed in | StackView** option from Xcode's **Editor** menu; it allows us to select some views and just wrap them into a stack view automatically. A shortcut to this method is the button **Stack** in the right-hand corner of interface editor in IB.

Now that we have a stack view with some subviews, it is time to define how we want these views to be displaced. From the attribute editor of the stack view, we get access to a number of important properties that we can use to change the stack view's behavior.

Axis, or the `axis` property (`UILayoutConstraintAxis`), defines the orientation (**Vertical** or **Horizontal**) of the arranged views in the stack view:

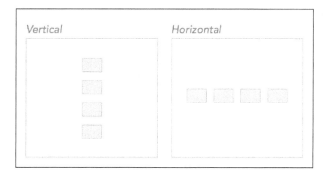

The alignment option, or the `alignment` property (`UIStackViewAlignment`), defines how the views are aligned inside the stack view's space. This property depends on the axis. For the vertical axis, we can align the elements to the **Leading**, **Center**, or **Trailing** alignments; for the horizontal axis, we can choose between the **Top**, **Center**, and **Bottom** positions. For both axes, we have the **Fill** option that, instead of aligning elements on a precise point, allows us to have them fill all the available space.

The stack view behavior can be even better defined through other properties that add more information to the layout.

The distribution option, or the `distribution` property (`UIStackViewDistribution`), defines how the elements are distributed in the stack view's available space. We might want to have the objects equally distributed throughout the entire space or just proportionally arranged depending on their intrinsic content sizes, with hugging or compression resistance. The main difference between these two methods is that with the latter, we change the size of the stack view elements, while with the former, the original object size is maintained, changing only the object's position through the stack's space.

The available values for this property are *fill, fill proportionally, fill equally*, which may change the elements' sizes, and *equally spacing* and *equally center*, which change only the elements' positions.

We can also force a minimum distance between elements with the `spacing` property that accepts `CGFloat` and tries to set a fixed gap among the arranged views.

All the views that are handled by the stack view are grouped in the `arrangedSubviews` array, which is a *subset* of the subviews of the stack view. We might want to add subviews to a stack view and be responsible for their placement in order to add decoration views, for example. These views are added using the normal `addSubview` methods, and they are not inserted into the `arrangedSubviews` array. This means that their constraints are not automatically created for you.

To programmatically add an arranged subview, call the `addArrangedSubview:` method, and to remove it, call `removeArrangedSubview:`. Remember that the view will only be removed from the `arrangedSubviews` group while it will still be available as a regular subview of the stack. To completely remove the view, call the `removeFromParent` method from the subview itself, as usual.

The UIStackView class is conceived as a container, so it can be considered a nonrendering subclass of UIView. Its only duty is to arrange a set of specific subviews. All the methods and properties related to drawing are not used (think of backgroundColor and drawRect as examples), making the stack view instances lightweight and fast.

It is important to note that the constraints needed to organize the content of the stack view are handled by the stack view itself. However, we are responsible for setting up the constraints to define how the stack view is placed inside its parent (unless its parent is another stack view).

UIStackView and adaptive layouts

All the properties we mentioned before are capable of handling different size classes. As you know by now, you can define constraints so that they are available for specific size classes only. The same is true for the axis, alignment, distribution, and spacing of the stack view properties.

From the attributes editor, to the right of these properties, you can find the "+" button that we saw while talking about constraints. With this button, you can specify all the combinations of size classes and property values that you need.

An interesting example is a stack view that uses a horizontal axis for a compact height and a vertical axis for a regular height. You can programmatically achieve this result just by overriding traitCollectionDidChange: and updating the axis property depending on the current verticalSizeClass value. You can do this by executing the following code:

```
override func traitCollectionDidChange(previousTraitCollection:
    UITraitCollection?) {

    UIView.animateWithDuration(1.0) { () -> Void in
        if self.traitCollection.verticalSizeClass == .Compact {
            self.stackView.axis = .Horizontal
        }else{
            self.stackView.axis = .Vertical
        }
    }
}
```

Another great feature of stack views that comes in handy when working with different size classes is the ability to hide one or more arranged views through the `hidden` property of `UIView` and immediately have all the other visible arranged views reorganized automatically. If you wrap the hide/unhide code within a `UIView` animation code (you will learn more about animation in the next chapter), all the views are nicely repositioned with a smooth animation.

Summary

With this chapter, you learned how to handle different screens with the same underlying code. You now have all the instruments you need to easily manage iOS 9 iPad's multitasking interfaces and, in general, those entire user interfaces that need to be heavily dynamic.

In the next chapter, you will learn how to animate user interface elements, and we'll talk about core animation, a lower-level framework that is used to draw most UIKit components under the hood.

6
Layers and Core Animation

Despite its name, *core animation* is much more than just animation. At the core of this framework, there is the CALayer class that, as we'll discuss in this chapter, is fundamental for the UIView class as a "presenter" for any view's drawing operation.

In this chapter, you'll learn how to work with layers and perform simple and complex animations with core animation and the UIView helper functions.

Exploring layers

Layers are behind almost all the views you encounter in iOS, and they are the very base of anything you do with core animation.

The CALayer class represents layers, and their main role is presenting content in a lightweight mode. The content is almost never drawn by the layer itself, but it is received as a bitmap, cached in a backing store, and then presented. You should look at layers as model objects rather than drawing elements; if there are any exceptions, it's probably because layers store the information needed to present some content generated somewhere else.

Layers and views

When a UIView class is instantiated, it sets its layer property with an instance of CALayer that, under the hood, contains a *backed* bitmap version of the view. This method ensures an efficient and lightweight solution to draw and animate contents.

A relationship between the layer and view is immediately created during initialization, and the view becomes the *delegate* of the layer. From now on, a view behaves similarly to a sort of wrapper for its layer. You'll learn more about all the layer properties in the next paragraphs, but here's a very simple example: when you change the `alpha` property on a view, you automatically change the `opacity` value for the main view layer. This relation ensures that you can easily update the view's properties without touching the underlying layer at all. You are obviously also allowed to access this layer if you need more control.

By default, the `layer` property instantiates a `CALayer` object. A different layer can be defined for a `UIView` subclass by simply overriding the `layerClass` static function and returning a different layer type or any custom `CALayer` subclass, as follows:

```
override class func layerClass() -> AnyClass {
    return MyLayer.self
}
```

A big difference between layers and views is that a layer is only used to manage and visualize content. A `UIView` instance is a subclass of `UIResponder`, and therefore it handles the event delivery through the responder chain (as you'll note in the next chapter). On the other hand, layers don't care about touches and events at all.

The content of a layer

The `CALayer` class is the base class for all the layer types you can create. A basic layer can be created through the `init` initialize, the `bounds/frame/position` properties are used to define the position and size of the layer, and the layer is attached to a super layer through the `addSublayer` function, exactly as happens with a view and its superview.

With these simple steps, we can create a basic contentless layer. Some other steps are needed to define what our layer shows. Let's examine all the available ways to set up the content of a layer.

Flat layer

In its simplest form, a layer can be drawn without specifying any content. Some of the properties of the layer can be used to draw a single-color surface. The `backgroundColor` property works exactly as it works for `UIView`. You can assign `CGColorRef` to this property, and this color will be used to tint the entire layer.

Another visual information that can be defined through properties is the layer's border; you can add a stroke to the bounds of a layer by assigning `CGColorRef` to the `borderColor` property and defining a `borderWidth`.

Here is an example that creates a gray layer with a two-point wide black border:

```
var layer = CALayer()
layer.bounds = CGRect(x: 0, y: 0, width: 100, height: 100)
layer.backgroundColor = UIColor.grayColor().CGColor
layer.borderColor = UIColor.blackColor().CGColor
layer.borderWidth = 2.0
```

The contents property

This is probably the easiest way to provide actual content to the layer: the `contents` property can be filled directly with an image reference. The image will be then presented with the help of some other properties, which give specific information about how the layer content has to be drawn (that is, the position, scale mode, and masks). All these properties are listed later in this chapter. Take a look at the following line:

```
layer.contents = UIImage(named: "Image")?.CGImage
```

> The image should be `CGImageRef`. Don't forget to convert `UIImage` before assigning it to `contents`. This property accepts `AnyObject` as input, and Xcode would not complain if you pass `UIImage` — too bad the content won't ever be displayed.

The layer delegate

An indirect way to set the layer's content is assigning the operation to another object through delegation. The `delegate` property of a layer can be associated with an object that implements one of these methods:

Method	Description
displayLayer(layer:)	When it implements the displayLayer method, the delegated object declares that it will set the contents property for the received layer within the execution of this method. The delegate becomes responsible for obtaining CGImageRef and setting it as the content for the layer.

Method	Description
`drawLayer(layer:inContext:)`	This method defines the content with a totally different approach; instead of assigning a value to the `contents` property, the `drawLayer` function is responsible for drawing directly inside the graphic context that is passed through the function itself. Core animation creates just an empty bitmap for the layer, and you can draw in it using core graphics. (A complete core graphics introduction is available as the last chapter of this book, don't worry.)

The delegate object implements `CALayerDelegate`, which is an *informal protocol*. What this means is that this protocol doesn't exist in the core animation framework. It is just available inside the documentation. The two methods previously described are added to the `NSObject` class through an extension available in the core animation headers.

Layer subclassing

As previously discussed, a layer doesn't normally draw its content by itself. There are, of course, methods that can be overridden to change this behavior. By creating a subclass of `CALayer` (or any other layer class), you will be able to provide a custom implementation of the drawing methods used by the layer. These methods are somehow similar to the methods listed in the delegate example, but they work directly with the layer:

Method	Description
`display()`	When we implement the `display` method, the layer class declares that it will set the `contents` property within the execution of this method. The layer becomes, therefore, responsible for obtaining `CGImageRef` and setting it as content.
`drawLayerInContext(ctx:)`	This method defines the content with a totally different approach. Instead of assigning a value to the `contents` property, the `drawLayerInContext` function is responsible for drawing directly inside the graphic context of the layer.

The methods presented in the delegation and subclassing steps are automatically called by the system; you don't call any of these methods manually. If the content of the layer needs to be updated, you can flag the layer as "update needed", calling the `setNeedDisplay` function of `CALayer`. Then, during the next drawing cycle, the content will be generated again from one of the previously listed methods.

The `displayLayer` and `display` methods have priority over the `drawLayer` and `drawLayerInContext` methods, which are called only if the other two are not implemented.

Contents properties

By default, when content is added to a layer, it is resized to fill all the available layer area. This behavior is not always a good solution, though. Thanks to the `contentsGravity` property, you have a finer control over the way content is displayed within the layer. This property expects a `String` variable that identifies one of the possible drawing modes.

These modes are grouped in two families: with the first, you define only the position of the content without changing its size. Some of the possible values for this family are `kCAGravityCenter`, `kCAGravityTop`, and `kCAGravityLeft`. The next image shows a complete list of the possible values:

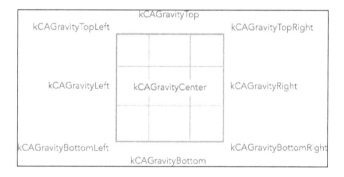

With the second family, the content size is updated to fit the layer area. In this case, you can choose from one of these values: `kCAGravityResize`, `kCAGravityResizeAspect`, and `kCAGravityResizeAspectFill`. The main difference between these last values and the previous ones lies in the way content is resized to fit the layer bounds.

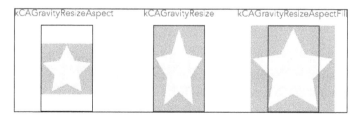

Another element that is extremely useful in defining how the layer content is drawn is the contentScale property. With this property, you can define the scale of the content depending on the screen's scale factor. With a regular retina display, the contentScale property for a layer is 2.0, while if the application is running on iPhone 6 Plus, the correct value is 3.0.

These numbers are obviously related to the size of the image that you are passing as content. If your layer is attached to a view, the contentScale value is handled for you according to the current screen scale factor.

The layer geometry

A layer is similar to a view to a certain extent: they share a lot in the way geometry is handled, and therefore, most of the properties available for views are also available for layers.

The most similar properties are probably frame and bounds. They work exactly the same way, defining the position and size of the layer in its context and super layer. On the other hand, while a layer cannot count on the center property, the position parameter can be considered really similar to this missing property. It accepts a CGPoint value, but instead of being an isolated value, it works in conjunction with another property — anchorPoint.

Defining the position property of a layer without considering the anchorPoint value is exactly the same as working with the center property of a view; the layer center is placed at the defined CGPoint value relative to its parent.

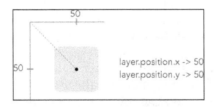

The anchorPoint value defines how the position is calculated and is placed at the center of the layer by default. It can be moved to a different position defined by a CGPoint value normalized to 1, whereas 0.5 identifies the center for both the x and y coordinates.

Using an arbitrary value, such as anchor point, you can change the way position and other operations such as *scaling* and *rotation* are calculated. The next image describes how the anchor point can alter this behavior:

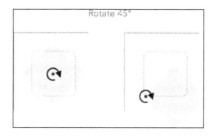

It is worth noting that the zPosition property can be used to define the drawing order of a layer along the z-axis as well. The value is equal to 0 by default. In a normal condition, without the intervention of other transformations, a layer will be drawn above a layer with a lower zPosition value.

Some interesting transformations can be applied to a layer and its sublayers in both 2D and 3D space. The transform property receives a transformation matrix handled by a CATransform3D structure. The logic behind the transformation matrix is outside the scope of this book, but don't worry; core animation provides a complete set of functions that you can use to create and handle transformation matrices for all the space transformations: *translate*, *rotate*, and *scale*.

The following example rotates and scales the layer using some of these methods:

```
let scale = CATransform3DMakeScale(3.0, 3.0, 0)
let scaleAndRotate = CATransform3DRotate(scale, 1.28, 0.0, 0.0, 1.0)
layer.transform = scaleAndRotate
```

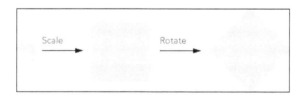

Let's have a quick look at the functions used to perform this transformation: the scale matrix is created using the CATransform3DMakeScale function, which receives values for the x, y, and z scales and returns a CATransform3D structure. In this example, we are interested in scaling the layer to three times its size on the *x*- and *y*-axes.

The scaleAndRotate matrix is created using a slightly different solution. As we already have a matrix that performs scale transformation, we want to keep this matrix and add another matrix that performs the rotation. The CATransform3DRotate function calculates the final CATransform3D structure, starting from the scale matrix and passing the values needed for the rotation (in the example, the layer is rotated by 1.28 radiant on the z-axis).

These functions can be organized in two different types, accounting for all the possible transformations:

Function	Description
`CATransform3DMake<Scale,Translate,Rotate>`	This creates a `CATransform3D` structure that describes a scale, translate, or rotate transformation.
`CATransform3D<Scale,Translate,Rotate>`	This creates a `CATransform3D` structure that describes a scale, translate, or rotate transformation, starting from an existing `CATransform3D` structure.

The `CATransform3DIdentity` matrix is a special matrix that describes the nontransformed state. This could be the value assigned to the transformation matrix when no transformations are applied, and it is really useful during animations. You can, for example, perform a two-step animation by applying the `scaleAndRotate` matrix first and then `CATransform3DIdentity` in order to bring the layer back to its original state. You'll read more about animations later in this chapter.

The layers hierarchy

Like views, layers can be organized in complex hierarchy structures by defining relationships and adding or removing objects. A layer can only have a single parent referenced by the `superlayer` property and many child layers that are listed within the `sublayers` property.

Here are some useful `CALayer` methods that come in handy to manage the hierarchy:

- The `addSublayer(_:)` function inserts a layer above the other sublayers of the new parent.
- You can gain finer control over the insertion process using `insertSublayer(_:atIndex:)` to define a specific index at which to insert the layer or using functions that add the layer relatively to other sibling layers, such as `insertSublayer(_:above:)`, `insertSublayer(_:below:)`, or `replaceSublayer(_:with:)`.
- The listing order of the layers in the sublayers array defines the drawing order. Layers at higher indices are drawn above lower indices (remember that you can also use the `zPosition` property to control the drawing order).

- You can call `removeFromParent()` from the layer itself to detach a layer from the hierarchy (this method is preferred over removing the layer from the sublayers property).

The appearance of layers

Some properties of the `CALayer` class can be used to change the aspect of the layer. We already introduced a couple of these properties, such as `backgroundColor`, `borderColor`, `borderWidth`, `contentsGravity`, and `opacity`, but many other options are available!

The `cornerRadius` property is particularly useful to create rounded layers. If used in conjunction with `masksToBounds`, you can hide content that is designed outside the layer area, thus obtaining some really nice effects.

A completely configurable shadow can be applied to any layer. The parameters in charge of handling the shadow are `shadowColor`; `shadowOffset`, which sets the direction of the projection; `shadowOpacity`; `shadowRadius`, which changes the size of the shadow; and even a custom `shadowPath`, which allows you to define a custom shape for the shadow:

Another interesting ability of layers is *masking*. This property is really useful to perform "revealing" animations or, more broadly, to achieve some complex designs.

Creating a mask for a layer is extremely easy; all you have to do is assign a layer to the `mask` property. The nontransparent pixels of the layer reveal the underlying original layer, while the transparent pixels don't.

CALayer is the base class for many other layer types available in core animation, such as CAGradientLayer, CAShapeLayer, and CATextLayer. These classes define custom properties, and they have really specific roles, but the bases you learned in the previous paragraphs are shared between all the available layer types.

Working with core animation

Core animation is a graphic and animation system that is adopted by iOS to draw and animate visual elements of the user interface. With this framework, the frame-by-frame operations are dramatically simplified by predefined structures and functions, which work as wrappers for complex processes that take place on the graphic hardware.

Layers and animations

The documentation of the CALayer class or any of its subclasses offers a list of properties that are marked in the description with the *animatable* keyword. This tag obviously means that a property can be animated; some examples of these properties are position and backgroundColor. These properties can be animated from the current value to a defined final value.

You don't have to worry about how the whole animation is generated because core animation performs an *interpolation* from the initial to the final value, creating smooth and customizable animations for you.

As we saw earlier on, a layer is a model object that contains information about its own structure. During the animation, this structure, which is also known as **model layer**, doesn't change. What is updated is a copy of the current model: the **presentation layer**.

Let's consider, for instance, animating the opacity of a layer. If you check for the opacity value during the animation, you'll find that it doesn't reflect what is shown on screen. To obtain the current animated value, you need to look at the opacity of the presentation layer. Both the model and presentation structures can be respectively obtained from the modelLayer (this is more likely to be equal to the original layer structure) and presentationLayer property. Execute the following code:

```
layer.presentationLayer().opacity
```

A third private structure takes part in this process by handling the lower-level operations with the graphic hardware during animation.

Implicit animations

The easiest way to obtain the animation of an `animatable` property is changing the value of this property at runtime. This action creates an animation that is attached to the layer and executed in the next drawing cycle. The animation is performed using default parameters and timing defined by iOS, and the changed value is updated both in the presentation layer and in the layer object's data.

This automatic behavior is implemented by core graphics thanks to the `CAAction` protocol, which is basically an interface that allows an object to trigger actions after any layer change. When one of these actions is triggered, core animation creates an object instance of `CATransaction` that animates the change. So, if you wish to avoid implicit animation for some property changes, you can manually disable the execution of transactions using this code:

```
CATransaction.begin()
CATransaction.setValue(kCFBooleanTrue, forKey:
kCATransactionDisableActions)
layer.backgroundColor = UIColor.redColor().CGColor
CATransaction.commit()
```

Properties animations

Implicit animations are a really effective solution if you want to animate quickly and with just a few lines of code. They are not the way to go if you want to achieve complex customized animations, though. In this case, you should rely on *explicit* animations. The `CAAnimation` class is an abstract class that provides basic support to perform animations on layer properties. You'll hardly handle this class directly, and generally, you'll work with one of the subclasses that are implemented in core animation.

The `CABasicAnimation` class is one of these subclasses, and as the name suggests, it is the right choice when performing basic animations of layer properties. Let's start with a simple example to learn how this class works.

Open the project for this chapter and have a look around; there's a simple environment created ad hoc. The `viewDidLoad` function in the `ViewController.swift` file instantiates a `CALayer` class called `roundedLayer`. We will use this layer to implement the examples of the coming pages.

In this first exercise, we animated a layer position, thus showing how the animation can be improved just using different parameters of the CABasicAnimation class, one step at a time.

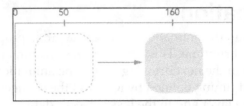

Initializing and launching the animation

A CABasicAnimation instance can be created and associated with a layer with a few lines of code, as follows:

```
let animation = CABasicAnimation(keyPath: "position.x")
animation.fromValue = 60
animation.toValue = 150
animation.duration = 0.5

roundedLayer.addAnimation(animation, forKey: "BasicAnimation")
```

Let's discuss the code line by line before adding it to the animateLayer function and launching the application to see the result.

The initialization is straightforward; we will pass the path for the property that we want to animate in the initializer (in this case, the x coordinate of position).

 Core animation extends the NSKeyValueCoding protocol by adding the key path support to CALayer in order to easily access CGPoint, CGRect, CGSize, and CATransform3D properties. This is why you can pass the key path to the initializer with the "position.x" form.

With the fromValue and toValue functions, we can specify the start and end points of the animation. Core graphics calculate the interpolation between these two points relative to the specified duration.

The duration value describes the time it will take to move the layer from the current x position to the final one. In other words, it is the duration of the animation expressed in seconds.

The last operation consists of adding the animation to the layer through the `addAnimation(_:forKey:)` function. The `forKey` parameter is an arbitrary name that you can assign to the animation. You might find this key useful later to retrieve the animation from the layer.

Keeping the animation result

As soon as you tap the "Animate!" button, the `animateLayer` function will start the animation, and the layer will move to the right of the screen. Somehow unexpectedly, when the animation completes, the layer will jump back to its initial position.

This behavior is related to the presentation and model layers we described before. During animation, the presentation layer position's value changes, but the data of the layer does not. As soon as the animation is completed, the presentation layer is cleaned and the layer jumps back to its original position.

You can instruct the animation to keep its final state by assigning the `kCAFillModeForwards` value to the `fillMode` property and constraining the animation on the layer by setting the animation the `removeOnComplete` property to `false`, as follows:

```
animation.fillMode = kCAFillModeForwards
animation.removedOnCompletion = false
```

The animation will now be completed, and the layer will keep its final position. It is important reiterate one point: what you are seeing on screen is just a representation of the presentation layer. If you try to access the position property of the layer data model now, you will get the initial position of the layer and not what you are seeing on screen.

An alternative solution if we want to keep the model and presentation layers synchronized is setting the property on this layer too. We will execute the following code for this:

```
// Set the model
roundedLayer.position.x = 150

// Perform the animation
let animation = CABasicAnimation(keyPath: "position.x")
animation.fromValue = 60
animation.toValue = 150
animation.duration = 0.5

roundedLayer.addAnimation(animation, forKey: "Move")
```

In this case, the layer doesn't start the implicit animation after `assigning150` to "x" because we will define a specific animation for the "position.x" key path within the same drawing cycle.

Handling timing and repetitions

With the `timingFunction` parameter, you can easily adjust the way the transition from the initial to final value is interpolated. The animation is executed with a linear function by default. With this function, the transition between the two points is executed with a linear acceleration. If you want to obtain a more dynamic animation, you can use an ease-in function. The animation will start slowly and accelerate towards the end in a really smooth way. Here is the code to obtain this result:

```
animation.timingFunction = CAMediaTimingFunction(name:
kCAMediaTimingFunctionEaseIn)
```

This property accepts instances of `CAMediaTimingFunction`. All the predefined values for this class are described in the following table:

Value	Description
`kCAMediaTimingFunctionLinear`	The animation starts and ends at the same speed.
`kCAMediaTimingFunctionEaseIn`	The animation starts slowly and accelerates until the end.
`kCAMediaTimingFunctionEaseOut`	The animation starts at a regular speed and decelerates around the end.
`kCAMediaTimingFunctionEaseInEaseOut`	The animation starts slowly, accelerates toward the midpoint of its duration, and decelerates until the end.
`kCAMediaTimingFunctionDefault`	The animation uses the curve used by the system's animations.

Even if they are not strictly related to `timingFunction`, there are other parameters implemented with the `CAMediaTiming` protocol that can alter the timing of the animation. The `beginTime` property defines a specific time at which to launch the animation. The `timeOffset` property receives an integer that describes the seconds of delay before starting the animation, and the `speed` parameter works in conjunction with the duration to locally define the real duration of the animation (an animation with *duration* = 2.0 and *speed* = 2.0 has an actual duration of 1.0).

A special behavior can be associated with an animation to repeat the transition from the initial to the final value more than once. The repeatCount value indicates the number of times an animation should be repeated. If we set a value of 2, the animation is repeated twice, starting from the initial value up to the end value, jumping back to the initial value, completing until the end a second time and jumping back again.

The next image describes the movements of the layer:

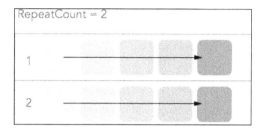

Depending on the result you want to achieve, a smoother way to repeat the animation might be what you need. If the autoreverse property is set to true, instead of jumping from the final to the initial value, the animation automatically executes an auto-reverse interpolation, thereby just reversing the animation's direction.

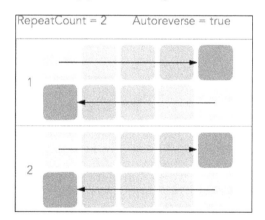

Here is the updated code that performs an auto-reversed and repeated animation:

```
let animation = CABasicAnimation(keyPath: "position.x")
animation.fromValue = 60
animation.toValue = 200
animation.duration = 0.5

animation.timingFunction = CAMediaTimingFunction(name:
kCAMediaTimingFunctionEaseInEaseOut)
```

```
animation.fillMode = kCAFillModeForwards
animation.removedOnCompletion = false

animation.repeatCount = 3
animation.autoreverses = true

roundedLayer.addAnimation(animation, forKey: "Move")
```

Animations group

With a basic animation, you can only obtain the animation of a single property at a time. An animation group gives you the ability to merge together more than one animation, thus mixing the final result in a single smooth animation.

CAAnimationGroup is a subclass of CAAnimation, so it can be handled exactly as a single animation. An instance of the group even has the same properties previously listed for CABasicAnimation. This is a great simplification that gives you the ability to manage multiple animations as a single one.

Let's create a group of animations. Remember that you can add the following code inside the animateLayer function of the project for this chapter and then compile and run to see the result. With this example, we will launch two different animations on roundedLayer. One will transform the dimension of the layer and the other the opacity, ending in a sort of "heartbeat" effect animation.

Here is the scaling animation:

```
let scaleAnimation = CABasicAnimation(keyPath: "transform")
let scale = CATransform3DMakeScale(0.5, 0.5, 1.0)
scaleAnimation.fromValue = NSValue(CATransform3D:
CATransform3DIdentity)
scaleAnimation.toValue = NSValue(CATransform3D: scale)
scaleAnimation.duration = 0.5
```

You already know how this code works, but there is an interesting thing to note. The CATransform3D matrix associated with the fromValue and toValue properties is translated to NSValue. You cannot pass a data structure as a value for a key, so if you want to use the CGPoint, CGRect, CGSize, or CATransform3D structures, you have to convert them into NSValue before assigning these values to the animation's properties.

The opacity animation is straightforward, as follows:

```
let opacityAnimation = CABasicAnimation(keyPath: "opacity")
opacityAnimation.fromValue = 1
opacityAnimation.toValue = 0
opacityAnimation.duration = 0.5
```

We can now create the animation group, fill its animation property with the animation previously created, and define some other properties, such as duration and repeat. Here's how:

```
let group = CAAnimationGroup()
group.animations = [opacityAnimation, scaleAnimation]
group.duration = 0.5
group.repeatCount = 2
group.autoreverses = true

roundedLayer.addAnimation(group, forKey: "Heart")
```

As you can see, the animation group can be added to the layer as a normal animation.

The animation duration will be clipped by the group animation by default. If you don't want to obtain unexpected results, it is good practice to define the duration and timing information at the group level.

Keyframe animations

All the animations that we discussed until now have an element in common: they go only through two steps, the initial and final values. More complex flows can be defined with keyframe animations. No longer constrained by just two steps, an animation can go through different states (the keyframes), each of them having completely different values.

The CAKeyframeAnimation class is another subclass of CAAnimation, and it works similarly to a basic animation. The only difference is obviously in the way you set the values for each keyframe. The properties of the animation responsible for this task are values and keyTimes, which are two arrays that contain the same number of elements and define the value and timing for each keyframe.

With the following code, we will change the backgroundColor property of roundedLayer passing through four different colors (red, green, blue, and yellow) to create a sequence of colors:

```
// keyframe animation
let animation = CAKeyframeAnimation(keyPath: "backgroundColor")
animation.fillMode = kCAFillModeForwards
animation.removedOnCompletion = false
animation.duration = 5

// Define the Keyframes
animation.values = [roundedLayer.backgroundColor,
                    UIColor.greenColor().CGColor,
```

```
                          UIColor.blueColor().CGColor,
                          UIColor.yellowColor().CGColor]
        animation.keyTimes = [0, 0.2, 0.8, 1]

        // Attach the animation
        roundedLayer.addAnimation(animation, forKey: "Colors")
```

The `values` property contains the list of colors for the sequence in the order that we want them to be shown in the animation. The `keyTimes` instance contains `CGFloat` values from `0` to `1`, where `0` identifies a point in time at the start of the animation, and `1` identifies a point at the end. This value is then translated in seconds according to the duration of the animation. Given the previous list of colors, the keyframes are built by associating the first element in `keyTimes` with the first element in the `values` array. Take a look at the following table:

Key time	Value	Time
0	Current background color	0 sec
0.2	Green color	duration * 0.2 = 1 sec
0.8	Blue	duration * 0.8 = 4 sec
1.0	Yellow	5 sec

The `roundedLayer` background color now smoothly changes to green during the first second of the animation. In the next 3 seconds (from 1 to 4 seconds), it animates to blue, and then it takes one last second to switch to yellow. If you change the duration of the animation, the timing will proportionally change.

Removing animations from a layer

When an animation is attached to a layer, it normally runs until the end of its cycle, or it repeats multiple times, depending on its settings. To remove an animation from a layer before its completion, you can refer to the key indicated with the `addAnimation(_:forKey:)` function.

The `removeAnimationForKey(_:)` function removes the animation previously added for the given key, as follows:

```
        roundedLayer.removeAnimationForKey("Move")
```

To remove all the animations at once, you can just call the `removeAllAnimation` method.

In both cases, the layer is immediately redrawn when the animation is removed. To avoid the layer jumping back to its initial state, you can retrieve the current presentation layer and override the layer data with the presentation layer data. Run the following script for this:

```
func removeColorsAnimation(){

    roundedLayer.backgroundColor =
            roundedLayer.presentationLayer().backgroundColor
    roundedLayer.removeAnimationForKey("Colors")
}
```

View animations

The `UIView` class provides some really useful helper functions that allow you to perform animations without working directly with the underlying layer. The easiest helper is the `animationWithDuration(_:animation:)` function. This method requires the duration of the animation and a closure of the `()->Void` type as parameters. With the closure code, you can programmatically define the animation by specifying the final value of the animated properties.

As an example, if you wanted to fade out a view, you would write `myView.alpha = 0` inside the closure. The `alpha` parameter for `myView` will be automatically animated as soon the animation gets executed. Take a look at the following code:

```
UIView.animateWithDuration(10){
    () -> Void in
    self.view.alpha = 0
}
```

The ability to animate views through closures is powerful; you are not limited to animating a single view at a time, and thanks to some more complex helpers, you can create even more interesting animations.

The `animationWithDuration(_:animation:completion:)` function lets you specify a closure that will be called at the end of the animation. This function can perform a sequence of animations because a second animation can be called inside the completion block itself. With this code, we will implement a typical *fadeOut-fadeIn* animation:

```
func fadeInFadeOut(){
    UIView.animateWithDuration(5, animations: { () -> Void in
        myView.alpha = 0
    }) { (completed) -> Void in
        UIView.animateWithDuration(2){
```

```
            () -> Void in
        otherView.alpha = 1
    }
  }
}
```

There is a helper method that you will surely love because it lets you implement spring animations without manually writing long keyframe sequences. A spring tries to jump back to its initial position, bouncing back and forth and progressively slowing down until it stops.

A really similar animation can be implemented with the `animateWithDuration(_:, delay:, usingSpringWithDamping:, initialSpringVelocity:, options:, animations:, complete:)` function.

By playing with `usingSpringWithDamping` and `initialSpringVelocity`, you can tweak the animations that, like the helpers we discussed previously, you write inside the closure. The final result will be that the values you animate (alpha, position, or any other `animatable` property) will change following a spring curve function. The best way to understand what you can create is probably to see this helper in action.

Here is an example that animates the vertical position of a view using the spring effect:

```
@IBAction func start(){

    UIView.animateWithDuration(1,
        delay: 0.0,
        usingSpringWithDamping: 0.8,
        initialSpringVelocity: 0.2,
        options: UIViewAnimationOptions.allZeros,
        animations: {
            () -> Void in
            self.v?.center.y += 250
        }) { (completed) -> Void in
            print("Animation completed!")
    }
}
```

Summary

With this chapter, you learned how layers and views work together in user interfaces, how to perform animations through core animation, and how easy it is to implement them with the `UIView` class helpers.

In the next chapter, you will learn how to add interactivity to a user interface and how touch events are handled by your custom views in general.

7
UI Interactions – Touches and Gestures

Users communicate with your interfaces through touch. Creating a responsive and strongly interactive user experience is, therefore, one of the keys to the success of your applications. In this chapter, you will learn how to handle all data exchanged with your app via the touchscreen, how to convert it into information that can be handled by your code, and how to launch activities in response to user interaction.

Events and touches

The events managed by iOS during user interaction are grouped into three main sets:

- **Multitouch** events are generated by the interaction with the screen
- **Motion** events are sensed by the accelerometer
- **Remote-control** events are mostly originated by external accessories

Even if these events are extremely different, they can be encapsulated and handled by the same class: UIEvent. An event instance can be easily distinguished by checking its type property, a UIEventType enum, with the following declaration:

```
enum UIEventType : Int {
    case Touches
    case Motion
    case RemoteControl
}
```

When users interact with the screen, a *multitouch* sequence is generated. Each step of a sequence is described by the same `UIEvent` instance that carries a set of `UITouch` objects: one per each of the user's fingers taking part in the multitouch sequence.

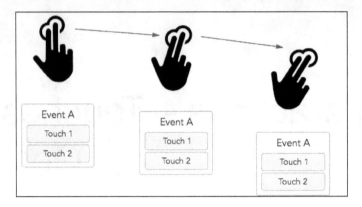

The event instance remains the same for the whole sequence, and the same is true for the touch instances that are updated during the sequence, preventing any waste of resources.

Touch phases

A multitouch sequence happens in different phases related to finger activity: as soon as the user touches the screen, the sequence *begins*. When fingers are *moving* or *stationary* on the screen, the sequence is updated. As soon as all the fingers leave the screen, the sequence *ends*. Any interrupting event (such as an incoming call) *cancels* the sequence.

Each of these phases generates an event that carries touch information. In turn, the `phase` property of the `UITouch` instance outlines the current phase with one of the possible values for the `UITouchPhase` enum type: `.Began`, `.Moved`, `.Stationary`, `.Ended`, or `.Cancelled`.

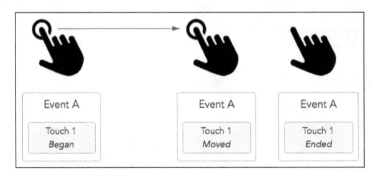

The UITouch class

As we discussed in the preceding section, the UITouch class handles all the activities for each single finger in a multitouch sequence. I believe it's important to have a quick overview of this class in order to understand which kind of information can be retrieved while working with its instances.

A touch takes place at a specific screen position, but you are more likely to get this location relatively to a view thanks to the locationInView(_:) method. This function receives a UIView instance and returns CGPoint, which is the location of the touch in the coordinate system of the given view (or window, if no views are passed to the function). Quite similarly, you can retrieve the touch position during the previous update phase with the previousLocationInView(_:) function.

 We already spoke about the phase property that identifies the phase of the touch in the current multitouch sequence.

The view property returns the view where the touch originally occurs. Keep in mind that this property doesn't necessarily describe the current view, considering that a user can start a touch in a view and end it in a different one. If you need it, you can also retrieve the initial window through the window property.

If a UITouch instance is handled by one or more gesture recognizers, the gestureRecognizers array contains references to these gesture recognizers. Later in this chapter, we'll discuss *gestures* in more detail.

The multitouch sequence is automatically managed by iOS to keep the sequence alive instead of ending it if subsequent taps happen within a short period of time. The total number of taps can be retrieved by the tapCount property of the touch instance.

A couple of interesting new features were added with *iOS 9* that allow us to work with *Touch3D*. The force property returns CGFloat, which describes how much the user has pressed on the screen to perform the current touch, and maximumPossibleForce, which identifies the maximum possible force value for the current device.

Other interesting features related to the brand new feature *Apple Pencil* are available from the UITouch class: altitudeAngle, for instance, is the angle of the pen in relation to the screen expressed in radians, where a value of *0* indicates that the stylus is parallel to the screen, while a value of *Pi/2* means that it is perpendicular.

Responder chain

An application can handle different kind of events thanks to *responder objects*. These objects implement specific methods that are useful to respond to one or more events. The UIResponder class is the base class where an interface for these events is defined; therefore, most of the classes that are directly exposed to user interaction are subclasses of UIResponder, such as UIView, UIViewController, UIControl, and even the UIApplication class.

A touch event is propagated through the application structure following an explicit path: the event is generated by the system and added into the *event queue*; the UIApplication singleton gets the topmost event and propagates it to the key window that, in turn, identifies the view where the touch occurred and passes the event to this view.

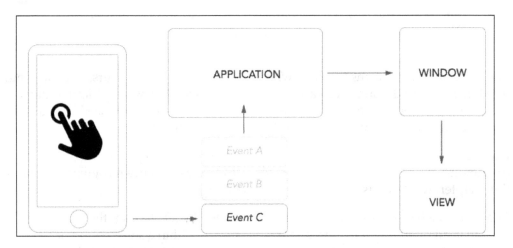

Hit-testing

The process through which this view is defined is called **hit-testing**, and it mainly relies on the hitTest(_:withEvent:) method. The logic is extremely simple: given a touch position, the hit-test checks whether this position intersects the bounds of a view, calling the pointInside(_:withEvent:) function on this view. If the function returns true, the process is repeated on the subviews of the view itself, and it is interrupted for a branch of the view hierarchy as soon as pointInside returns false. The deepest view in the hierarchy that responds true to the hit-testing is the view in which the event will be initially passed.

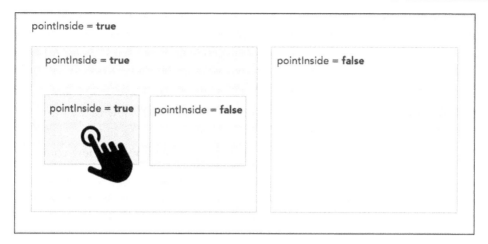

This process can exclude a view, and subsequently all its subviews, in different ways. The hitTest function automatically fails if the userInteractionEnabled property for a given view is set to false. The visibility properties, such as hidden and alpha, can also be used to exclude user interaction on a view; hiding a view with these properties is exactly the same as disabling user interaction.

A more aggressive way to completely avoid user interaction in the whole application is calling the beginIgnoringInteractionEvents function on the UIApplication object. You can then reestablish the normal interaction flow by calling endIgnoringInteractionEvents.

Responding to touch events

Now that a view is identified, it doesn't mean that it can also handle the touch event. We have only identified the initial point where we can look for a valid responder for the current touch event.

In order to become a valid responder for a touch event, an object has to implement four methods of the UIResponder class. These methods are strictly related to the touch *phases* previously described:

- touchesBegan(_,event:)
- touchesMoved(_,event:)
- touchesCancelled(_,event:)
- touchesEnded(_,event:)

By implementing these methods, the object declares that it is able to handle the event. If this is not the case, the event will be propagated to the *next responder* identified by the nextResponder() function. You are generally not required to override the nextResponder function. In fact, the general logics used to identify the next responder of the chain are defined for you by these simple rules:

- The next responder for a *view* that is not the topmost view of a view controller is its *superview*

- The next responder for a *view* that is the topmost view of a view controller is the *view controller*

- The next responder for a *view controller* is its *window*

- The next responder for a *view controller* that is a child of another view controller is its *parent view controller view*

- The next responder for a *window* is the *application singleton*

A simple implementation of these methods can be adopted with a UIView subclass to perform a drag and drop action:

```
override func touchesBegan(touches: Set<NSObject>, withEvent
  event: UIEvent) {
    super.touchesBegan(touches, withEvent: event)
    originalColor = backgroundColor
    backgroundColor = UIColor.yellowColor()
}

override func touchesMoved(touches: Set<NSObject>, withEvent
  event: UIEvent) {
    super.touchesMoved(touches, withEvent: event)

    var t = touches.first as? UITouch
    self.center = t!.locationInView(self.superview)
}

override func touchesCancelled(touches: Set<NSObject>!, withEvent
  event: UIEvent!) {
    super.touchesCancelled(touches, withEvent: event)
    backgroundColor = originalColor
}

override func touchesEnded(touches: Set<NSObject>, withEvent
  event: UIEvent) {
    super.touchesEnded(touches, withEvent: event)
    backgroundColor = originalColor
}
```

During the *begin phase*, this code keeps a reference of the original background color of the view and sets the new background color to yellow to warn the user that the drag operation has begun.

With the *move phase*, the center of the view is updated using the location of the touch in the superview that it was obtained with to the locationInView function. Since the touchesMoved function receives a set of touches that can contain information about one or more fingers, we can simplify the process by only keeping the *first* touch.

When the touch phase *ends* (or in case, is *cancelled*), the original background color is restored.

Gestures and gesture recognizers

Within the methods previously shown, you can perform complex operations and even programmatically filter the touch actions you want to handle, starting from the analysis of UITouch objects. Just to give you an example, you might be able to define that if the touch is constantly moving to the left of the screen in a considerable short amount of time, the user is performing a *swipe left* action. Identifying multitouch sequences as specific actions using only the UIResponder functions is not trivial, though—especially when it comes to multitouch sequences.

Luckily enough, iOS comes with a number of preset actions that we more appropriately call *gestures*. A gesture is a way to turn a touch sequence into a specific pattern thanks to algorithms that convert finger movements under the hood into a single specific action.

The set of gestures handled by iOS is somewhat small, but it includes most of the relevant movements you may need for your applications. Here they are:

Tap	This describes what we can easily refer to as a "mouse click" on a computer. It consists of single or multiple pokes on the screen and can be performed with one or more fingers.
Pan	This indicates that the user is moving one or more fingers around the screen without forming any specific pattern.
Pinch	This gesture is largely used to perform zoom operations on all the modern mobile devices. The pattern involves two touches (that is, fingers) that move toward or away from one other.
Rotate	Similar to the pinch gesture, this involves two touches that, this time, rotate in a circular motion around a shared pivot point while keeping the same relative distance.

Swipe	This gesture involves moving one or more fingers in an "easy-to-identify" direction, which may be left, right, up, or down.
Long press	This is the same as tap, but the fingers have to stay on the screen for a predefined minimum duration.

Working with gesture recognizers

Intercepting and isolating some of these sequences through UIResponder methods might be complicated. This is why iOS gives us a set of dedicated classes called **gesture recognizers** that come in handy to manage gestures and easily react to them.

A gesture recognizer works in conjunction with a view, leveraging the *target-action* pattern. A gesture recognizer is implemented by a subclass of the generic UIGestureRecognizer class. Depending on the gesture that you need to handle, you can initialize a gesture recognizer by choosing from among the following:

- UITapGestureRecognizer
- UILongPressGestureRecognizer
- UISwipeGestureRecognizer
- UIPinchGestureRecognizer
- UIPanGestureRecognizer
- UIRotateGestureRecognizer

The steps needed to set up and handle a gesture are straightforward:

1. Create a specific gesture recognizer for one of the gesture types, and specify the target and the action to be called when the gesture occurs through its initializer. Here's the code that you need to execute:

   ```
   var gesture = UITapGestureRecognizer(target: self, action:
      "tap:")
   ```

2. Attach the gesture recognizer to the view where the gesture can take place by calling the addGestureRecognizer(_:) method of UIView, as follows:

   ```
   myView.addGestureRecognizer(gesture)
   ```

In the previous example, the tap function will be called when a tap gesture is recognized on the myView view. The tap function will receive the gesture recognizer object with specific information related to the gesture. Each gesture recognizer class adds to the base UIGestureRecognizer class a list of properties that are strictly related to the gesture it represents.

For instance, you can retrieve the current `scale` value that increases or decreases based on the distance between the two fingers from a `UIPinchGestureRecognizer` instance.

Gesture recognizer states

A gesture recognizer defines its current state through a simple finite state machine. The possible values for its state are slightly different, depending on whether the gesture is *discrete* (that is, whether it is a single event, tap, long press, or swipe) or *continuous* (meaning it takes place over a period of time, such as pinch, rotate, and pan).

The possible states are *possible*, *began*, *changed*, *failed*, *ended*, and *cancelled*. The following figures describe the transitions between these states:

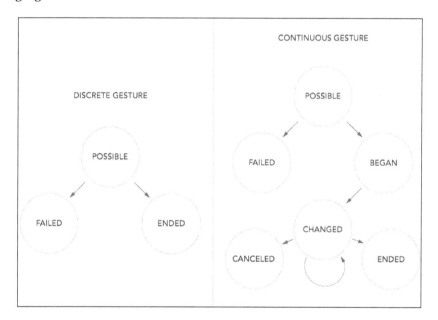

A discrete gesture can be *recognized (ended)* as a gesture, or it may transition to *failed* if no valid pattern is found. A continuous gesture passes through the *began* state when the gesture is first recognized and keeps the *changed* state while the gesture is in progress. It can transition to *cancelled* if the gesture is no longer a valid pattern, and finally, it goes to *ended* when a user's fingers detach from the screen.

The state of a gesture can be easily accessed through the *state* property that returns an enum of the `UIGestureRecognizerState` type.

Hands-on code

Let's complete this chapter by implementing a simple interface that gives to users the ability to scale a view thanks to gesture recognizers. You can open the `Start\Chapter7` project from the `Chapter7_Source_FD` folder for the initial setup, which consists of a view controller that programmatically adds a red view in the center of its topmost view.

We will start by initializing the gesture recognizer. A good place to perform this operation is in the view controller's `viewDidLoad` function; just after the code related to the `redView` initialization, run the following:

```
override func viewDidLoad() {
    super.viewDidLoad()

    // Initialize the redview
    redView = UIView(frame: CGRectMake(0, 0, 100, 100))
    redView?.backgroundColor = UIColor.redColor()
    redView?.center = view.center
    view.addSubview(redView!)

    // Initialize and attach the gesture recognizer
    let pinchGR =
    UIPinchGestureRecognizer(target: self, action: "pinch:")

    view.addGestureRecognizer(pinchGR)
}
```

Now, the whole view controller's main view can respond to pinch gestures through the `pinch` function. As the result, we want to apply a transformation to `redView`, depending on the pinch value. As you can note from the following code snippet, this is simple:

```
func pinch(gesture:UIPinchGestureRecognizer){

    // Handle different gesture states
    switch gesture.state {

        case .Began:
            redView?.layer.transform = CATransform3DIdentity

        case .Changed:
            //Apply transform
            var transform = CATransform3DMakeScale(gesture.scale,
              gesture.scale, 0)
```

```
            redView?.layer.transform = transform

        default:
            UIView.animateWithDuration(0.2, animations: {
                () -> Void in
                 self.redView?.layer.transform =
                   CATransform3DIdentity
            })
    }
}
```

We can perform different actions depending on the state of the gesture. The core of the function where the scale transformation is applied is within the .Changed case. The current scale gesture value is directly converted into CATransform3D and assigned to the layer's transform property.

The .Began case resets the transform property to CATransform3Didentity, and the default case does the same within an animation block. This means that when the user lifts his/her fingers, redView will jump back to its original size, performing a quick animation.

Summary

In this chapter, you learned the role of some important classes, such as UIResponder and UITouch. Now, you know how events are propagated through your view hierarchy and how you can improve user experience through gestures and touch handling.

In the next chapter, we will go another step further. It is finally time to create your very own custom control using many of the concepts that we went through so far and deal with the implementation of nontrivial user interfaces.

How to Build Custom Controls

8

In the previous chapters, you learned the basics needed to create user interfaces, starting from the huge set of elements provided by Apple itself. Sometimes, though, a particularly complex design or an unusual way required to interact with your app generates an equally unusual need that cannot be satisfied using the UIKit set only. In this chapter, you'll learn how to build a totally custom control by designing its structure and user interface and by programming all the functionalities from the ground up in order to create something that answers your specific need.

The Thermostat control

The **Internet of Things** (**IoT**) is a really fascinating field. New products are hitting the market every day, and mobile applications are exceptional candidates that provide alternative ways to control these objects. In this chapter, we will build our contribution to IoT by creating an interface that will allow us to send and receive commands from a *connected thermostat*. To be precise, we will implement a custom control similar to a slider that can be used to define a value on a predefined scale. This value can be greater than, less than, or equal to zero.

Here is a preview of our thermostat control slider:

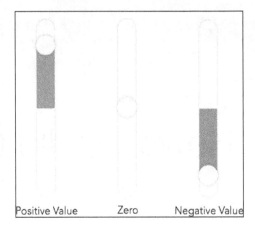

Positive Value   Zero   Negative Value

Designing a custom control

Before starting with the code itself, it is very strongly recommended (read mandatory) to plan and design the control that you want to build. This is probably the most important part of the whole process. Thanks to a good plan, you can evaluate case by case, which involves the real effort in going custom, and even define whether you actually need a custom component.

The first question you have to ask yourself or your team is, "Why do I need to build this?" You might come up with different answers: "I need a completely custom design for a control that already exists but can't be customized enough using the UIKit appearance only", "the functionalities and interactions that I need can't be handled by any other UIKit component", or even "I want to slightly modify a UIKit component that already exists, but my needs cannot be satisfied just by subclassing it". All these are valid answers that might lead you toward implementing your very custom control. So, what about the thermostat control? It's a slider, but we cannot build it just by starting from the default `UISlider` class and changing its appearance. For our case, we obviously need a custom control; even if the functionalities are really similar to an existent UIKit component, the design and interactions can't be easily reshaped to fit our needs.

The main role of a control is to convert user interactions into values or events. It is really important to be consistent with the type of response that you are planning for your control. Take your cue from a generic button and slider; with a button, the user can request a single action, or if the button is configurable enough, it can be used as a switch to set and get a dual value, such as on and off. With a slider, the user can set and get incremental numeric values.

The way users interact with these controls is completely different; they are planned to provide an intuitive interaction that allows them to get the expected result without thinking too much. Users should be guided by the design of the control, which in turn has to be clear and in line with the main guidelines proposed by Apple in order to ensure what is good *user experience*. For the thermostat control, we want to create something really similar to a default `UISlider` class so that our users immediately get how to use it. We can achieve this goal by implementing the same exact interaction driven by drag and drop and with a similar design. As soon as a user drags the handle, a track will be drawn imitating the default sliders. At this point, we will give users another hint in the form of different colors for the active track to represent hot and cold values. The only real differences between this and the default slider are the drag direction—vertical instead of horizontal—and the value zero, which is located at the center of the control instead of on its left-hand side.

An important aspect that needs to be addressed is the *reusability* of a component. If you want to create a really generic control that can be reused in different applications, you should plan and design it while trying to keep some of its elements easily customizable. On the other hand, if you are not planning to reuse the control, you don't have to spend too much effort trying to prematurely generalize the design or even the functionalities. For the example of this chapter, the only thing that we will keep generic is the tint of the hot and cold track. We'll use the UIKit appearance to achieve this goal.

The UIControl class

There are many different starting points for the creation of your component. If you take a look at some of the custom controls available online, you will find that you can even start from a `UIView` subclass and draw the control parts in its `drawRect` method. There isn't a "right way to do it", but in order to be consistent with `UIKit` controls and have some advantages during the control's implementation, starting with the `UIControl` class is definitely a good choice.

This class provides an interface for the common structure of a control. You cannot use it directly, but it has to be subclassed by overriding some main methods if you want to implement your custom functionalities.

The `UIControl` class is, in turn, a subclass of `UIView`, meaning that you will get all the functions available for the views and your control can be directly attached as a subview of the current user interfaces.

The functionalities provided by the UIControl class are obviously all about control behaviors. Take a look at the following list:

- The *target-action* pattern is at the core of the control messages' dispatch, and it is implemented in the UIControl class, providing some useful methods that simplify the way you handle targets for all the actions performed by the control. All the events (actions) that a control can dispatch, such as TouchUpInside, TouchDragInside and ValueChanged, are represented by the UIControlEvents structure. You can send an event to all the subscribed targets through the sendActionsForControlEvents(_:) method.

- Through the UIControlState enum, which is a list of possible states such as Normal, Highlighted, Disabled, and Selected, the UIControl class enables you to keep track of the *state* of the control. You are responsible for some of the states that depend on the behavior you want to design for the control.

- The *touch tracking* pattern is helpful in defining how users can interact with the control. Through a list of methods provided by the UIControl class, you can easily receive and handle touches that are directed to your control. You can implement all or some of these methods depending on your needs:

```
beginTrackingWithTouch(_:withEvent:) continueTracking
  WithTouch(_:withEvent:) endTrackingWithTouch
  (_:withEvent:) cancelTrackingWithEvent(_:)
```

The rest of this chapter is all about the implementation of the control. We will discuss how to define its behaviors in detail, leveraging on the properties and functionalities that we just saw.

Implementing the ThermostatSlider control

The first step is to subclass UIControl by creating a new file in Xcode and giving a name to the new class; ThermostatSlider sounds about right.

Note that at any time during the explanation, you can check the full source code to verify how to move from one step to the next one. During the chapter, we will describe only the key parts of the implementation.

A good practice that helps you keep your code clean is using the // MARK: comment to separate the projects in subsections. To be consistent with the chapter, the code that you'll find for this project is split into four main sections: *initialization*, *design*, *update*, and *touch tracking*. We will now examine them one by one.

Control initialization

It is good practice to keep the code readable and, when possible, split logics into simple independent functions. In some cases, writing comments is almost redundant; good code can be automatically documented using clear names for variables and methods. For our control, we want to somehow move in this direction; however, you don't have to worry because this chapter's code is documented with tons of comments. We'll just adopt a really clear naming convention and split logics into subfunctions.

The initialization of the controller is separated in to three methods that are responsible for the setup and drawing of the control components. We call these methods with the `init` function, as follows:

```
override init(frame:CGRect){

    super.init(frame:frame)

    designBorders()
    designTrack()
    designHandle()
}
```

At this stage, the geometries of the control and its parts are not defined yet. The bounds and frames for the control's parts are specified through other functions and called using `layoutSubviews` every time a layout update is required or when the current value of the control changes. Execute the following code:

```
override func layoutSubviews() {
    super.layoutSubviews()

    // Update Layers frames
    updateBorder()
    updateHandle()
    updateTrack()
}
```

The `design<Part>` and `update<Part>` methods will be explained in the next sections.

Drawing the control

The user interface for the thermostat control is really similar to a common slider, and it can be easily drawn using different parts.

Borders delimit the control area. The handle (or thumb) is the element that a user can drag around to change the current value, and the track is a colored line that is drawn inside the control to represent the currently selected value.

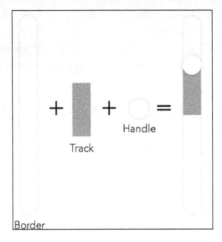

We use layers to draw these parts (you' learned a lot about layers in *Chapter 6, Layers and Core Animation*) by creating a simple hierarchy of elements.

Now that we know how the control should look, we can have some fun prototyping its design!

Prototyping using playground

Playground is a new welcome addition to Xcode that will help us during the design process. With this project type, we can easily prototype the design we want to create without the burden of a complete project.

You can create a new Playground project from the Xcode menu by navigating to **File | New | Playground**. Now, you should see an almost empty page that includes only the UIKit import and a UILabel definition. Delete the definition and keep only the UIKit import statement. The Playground is essentially a way to draw code and immediately look at the result of the code without compiling the project. Xcode 7 even added the ability to write markdown comments by importing external source code and having different pages for each Playground project. It keeps getting better.

Before prototyping the control parts, we need to perform a couple of adjustments. The first consists in activating the Playground "preview area" where the design will be shown. From the Xcode menu, navigate to **View | Assistant Editor | Show Assistant Editor**, and a new page area appears on the right-hand side of the code. We now have to create a sort of container where we will draw our prototypes. By default, a Playground doesn't come with a view that you can attach elements to, like a view controller, so we have to manually create this view and declare that we want to see it inside the Playground preview. We will execute the following code:

```
let containerView = UIView(frame: CGRect(x: 0.0, y: 0.0, width:
    320.0, height: 640.0))
XCPlaygroundPage.currentPage.liveView = containerView
containerView.backgroundColor = UIColor.whiteColor()
```

The `liveView` function is responsible for identifying the view that has to be added to the Playground timeline. The `containerView` function is now the main view of the hierarchy for our prototype, and we can use it as a white dashboard.

Drawing the borders

The layer that designs borders is extremely simple. We can start from a rectangle and obtain the "capsule" shape that represents the slider boundaries through the `cornerRadius` property, as follows:

```
let sliderFrame = CGRect(x: 100, y: 30, width: 30, height: 200)

let borderLayer = CALayer()
borderLayer.frame = sliderFrame

borderLayer.backgroundColor = UIColor.whiteColor().CGColor
borderLayer.borderColor = UIColor(white: 0.9, alpha: 1.0).CGColor
borderLayer.borderWidth = 1
borderLayer.cornerRadius = sliderFrame.size.width / 2.0
borderLayer.masksToBounds = true

containerView.layer.addSublayer(borderLayer)
```

For now, we will manually define the frame of the borders; later, we'll have the shape defined by Auto Layout. To be sure, the track layer doesn't exit the slider boundaries as we set `maskToBounds` to `true`. The layer is then attached to the container view. At this point, you should be able to see a preview of the layer to the right of the playground code area.

Drawing the track

This layer, together with the handle, is the part of the control that will be updated depending on the current value selected by the user. On your current Playground file, add this code to take a look at how the layer is drawn:

```
// Track Layer
let trackLayer = CALayer()

trackLayer.anchorPoint = CGPoint(x: 0.5, y: 1)
trackLayer.backgroundColor = UIColor.redColor().CGColor
trackLayer.frame = CGRect(x: 0, y: 0, width: 30, height: 80)
trackLayer.position = CGPoint(
    x: borderLayer.bounds.size.width/2,
    y: borderLayer.bounds.size.height/2)
borderLayer.addSublayer(trackLayer)
```

To simplify the placement of this layer, we will attach it as a centered sublayer of `borderLayer`. The current configuration will make the track grow upwards. To allow it to grow downwards, just change the anchor point by assigning 0 to the *Y* anchor value. This is exactly what we will do later when the height, direction, and color of the track will be defined by the current control value. Take a look at the following line of code:

```
trackLayer.anchorPoint = CGPoint(x: 0.5, y: 0)
```

Drawing the handle

Previously, we defined the border by making `maskToBounds` be equal to `true`. If we attached `handleLayer` as a child of `borderLayer`, we would probably experience some graphic glitches because some pixels of the handle may end up being masked. To avoid this problem, we can just draw the handle as a sibling of the border layer above it. We will round the layer shape using `roundCorner` to obtain a circle and apply a shadow to make the handle more visible.

Put this code in the Playground area to see the result (note that the handle position is not correct at the moment; we will just place it at the center of the control). Here's the code that needs to be executed:

```
let handleLayer = CALayer()

handleLayer.position = borderLayer.position
handleLayer.bounds.size = CGSize(
    width: borderLayer.bounds.size.width,
    height: borderLayer.bounds.size.width)
```

```
handleLayer.cornerRadius = borderLayer.bounds.size.width / 2.0

handleLayer.backgroundColor = UIColor.whiteColor().CGColor
handleLayer.shadowColor = UIColor.blackColor().CGColor
handleLayer.shadowOffset = CGSize(width: 0.0, height: 0.0)
handleLayer.shadowRadius = 2
handleLayer.shadowOpacity = 0.3
handleLayer.anchorPoint = CGPoint(x: 0.5, y: 0.5)

containerView.layer.addSublayer(handleLayer)
```

The layer size is strictly related to the `borderLayer` width. This choice ensures that any change to `borderLayer` doesn't break the design of the control. You can update the `borderLayer` size to take a look at how the control's design is nicely updated.

Updating the control value

The variable that keeps track of the current value is called _value. It is private and can be accessed through the `value` property with a dedicated getter and setter. Having a clear entry point for the value of the control is really useful because we can consequently update the current layout and filter inputs. Here is the full code of the `value` property:

```
var value:Float {
    get { return _value}
    set (newValue){

        // Filter input ----------------
        if newValue >= 0{
            _value = min(newValue, maxValue)
        }else{
            _value = max(newValue, -maxValue)
        }

        // update parts ----------------
        CATransaction.begin()
        CATransaction.setAnimationDuration(0)
        updateHandle()
        updateTrack()
        CATransaction.commit()

            self.sendActionsForControlEvents(UIControlEvents
              .ValueChanged)
    }
}
```

With the first lines of the setter, we filtered inputs that define that the value cannot be greater than the value defined by maxValue or lower than −maxValue (remember that the control value can be positive and negative). Then, we called the updateHandle and updateTrack functions to reset the layers' sizes and positions to reflect the new value. To avoid unwanted implicit animations, we adopted the CATransaction class. We'll get into the details of sendActionsForControlEvents later.

It is really important to define how the control represents the current selected value; in our case, the elements that take part in this process are essentially the handle and track layers. To be precise, for the handle, we updated its current Y position, while for the track, we updated the color, height, and anchor point. Let's proceed with implementing the necessary code to update the current state of these control parts.

Our control's design is already prototyped, so we can close Playground and move the code to the ThermostatSlider file. Some lines of the init<part> functions have to be moved to the update<part> relative functions. This is because the size of the elements depends on information defined through Auto Layout, and they are not available at the time of initialization. Let's go through the updated functions one by one.

Updating borders

The updateBorder function is only responsible for the updating of the borders' frames and the corner radius in relation to the bounds of the control. For instance, if Auto Layout is defined to resize the control when the device is rotated, the updateBorder function redesigns the current borders. Run the following code:

```
private func updateBorder(){

    borderLayer.frame = bounds
    borderLayer.cornerRadius = bounds.size.width / 2.0
}
```

Updating the track

The tracklayer frame must be redesigned after any value update and when the control is resized. On the contrary, the layer's color and anchor point are bound only to the current value. Execute the following script:

```
private func updateTrack(){

    // Update track size
    trackLayer.frame = CGRectMake(0, 0, self.bounds.width, 0)
    trackLayer.position = CGPoint(
        x: bounds.size.width/2,
```

```
        y: bounds.size.height/2)

    // Update layer height depending on value
    trackLayer.bounds.size.height = abs(valueToY())

    // Update anchor point and color depending on value
    if value >= 0{
        trackLayer.anchorPoint = CGPoint(x: 0.5, y: 1)
        trackLayer.backgroundColor = hotTrackColor.CGColor
    }else{
        trackLayer.anchorPoint = CGPoint(x: 0.5, y: 0)
        trackLayer.backgroundColor = coldTrackColor.CGColor
    }

}
```

The `trackLayer` position must be at the center of `borderLayer`. We can calculate this position using the control `bounds` size because `borderLayer` has exactly the same width and height of the whole control area.

The track height update is delegated to another single-role function: `valueToY`. This function, thanks to a simple proportion, is able to convert the current control value to a Y coordinate point on the track. This is done through the following code:

```
private func valueToY()->CGFloat{
    return CGFloat(value) / CGFloat(maxValue) *
    (bounds.size.height - handleLayer.bounds.size.height / 2.0) / 2.0
}
```

Here is a simple example: if the control has a height of 100 points, it has 50 points for the positive track and 50 for the negative. Given `maxValue` equals 10.0, to represent the value 5.0, the positive track has to fill half of the available space. In this case, the `valueToY` function will return 25.0, the value that has to be associated with the height of `trackLayer`.

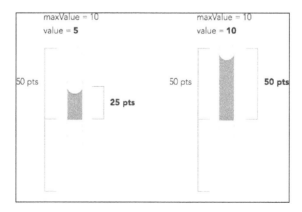

The last step of the `updateTrack` function consists of updating the color and anchor point of the layer. For positive control values, we will set the Y anchor point to 1 and the layer will grow from the center of the control to the top, while for negative values, the Y anchor point 0 just makes the layer grow from the center downwards.

Updating the handle

The `handleLayer` size, as we previously defined in the prototype, depends on the size of the control, while the position is obviously strictly related to the control's current value. The `updateHandle` function is responsible for setting the handle frame in relation to these elements. Execute the following code for this:

```swift
private func updateHandle(){

    // Update size and radius depending on control width
    let controlWidth = bounds.size.width

    handleLayer.bounds.size = CGSize(
        width: controlWidth,
        height: controlWidth)
    handleLayer.cornerRadius = controlWidth / 2.0

    // Update handle position depending on value
    var position = borderLayer.position
    if value != 0 {
        position.y -= valueToY()
    }
    handleLayer.position = position
}
```

The height and width of the handle are equal to the width of the control, and its corners will be completely rounded to obtain a circle. Initially, `handleLayer` is vertically and horizontally centered in the control using the position of `borderLayer` as a reference. Then, thanks to the `valueToY` function, the vertical position of the handle is updated to the right point.

Touch tracking

At this point, the control is able to autonomously design and update its parts to reflect the current value. This might be enough for a noninteractive control, responsible only for displaying information, but as we want to get input from users, we have to go one step further.

Users will interact with our control through touch; they can tap a specific point or drag the handle up and down. The UIControl class, as previously anticipated, provides four methods to fully handle this interaction.

Beginning tracking

As soon as a user touches the control, the beginTrackingWithTouch method is called. With this method, we will define that the control has to receive continuous touches, returning true. If this is not the case, only a single touch event is handled. Try to set the return value to false to note the difference; the handle will be placed at the touch location, but when you start dragging, nothing will happen.

We can manage all the initial setup to start the interaction. We will set the control's state to *highlighted* and perform an explicit animation to increase the size of the handle; finally, we will convert the user touch location to the current control value. We can do all this using the following script:

```
override func beginTrackingWithTouch(touch: UITouch,
withEvent event: UIEvent?) -> Bool{

    self.highlighted = true

    self.handleLayer.transform = CATransform3DMakeScale(1.5, 1.5, 1)

    let point = touch.locationInView(self)
    value = valueFromY(point.y)



    return true
}
```

The valueFromY function works similarly to valueToY; however, instead of taking the control value and returning a relative *Y* coordinate point, it takes a *Y* coordinate point and returns a control value. Take a look at the following:

```
private func valueFromY(y:CGFloat)->Float{

    let cleanY = min(max(0, y), bounds.size.height)

    let trackHalfHeight = bounds.size.height / 2.0
    let translatedY = trackHalfHeight - cleanY

    return Float(translatedY) * maxValue / Float(trackHalfHeight)
}
```

This function caps the minimum and maximum Y locations using the control bounds height as limit. The Y point is then translated into an easier-to-handle coordinate space that has the zero point at the center of the control. Finally, through a proportion, the translated point is converted to a valid value.

Continuing tracking

User touch actions are continuously passed to the control through the continueTrackingWithTouch function as we returned true in the previous function. With this, as long as we return true, we can keep converting the user touch location to a valid control value by adopting again the valueFromY function, as follows:

```
override func continueTrackingWithTouch(touch: UITouch, withEvent
event: UIEvent?) -> Bool {
    let point = touch.locationInView(self)
    value = valueFromY(point.y)

    return true
}
```

Ending tracking

When the interaction is stopped by a user or cancelled by the system, the endTrackingWithTouch or cancelTrackingWithEvent functions are called. Here, we have the chance to reset the control, removing the highlighted state and resizing the handle to its initial size. In general, this is the right place to remove any information you temporarily add through the tracking methods. Here's the code for this:

```
override func endTrackingWithTouch(touch: UITouch?, withEvent event:
UIEvent?) {
    self.handleLayer.transform = CATransform3DIdentity
    self.highlighted = false

}

override func cancelTrackingWithEvent(event: UIEvent?) {
    self.handleLayer.transform = CATransform3DIdentity
    self.highlighted = false
}
```

Sending actions

The `ThermostatSlider` implementation is almost complete; we are just missing a way to communicate the change of the current value, exactly as a common `UISlider` class does with the object subscribed to its value update.

The `UIControl` class provides methods to handle the *target-action* pattern in a really easy way; you can add a new target object with `addTarget(_:action:forControlEvents:)` specifying the action and event to which to subscribe. Then, you can remove this with the `removeTarget(_:action:forControlEvents:)` method. The list of targets subscribed to the control events can be retrieved using the `allTargets()` method. You can even obtain the name of the action called when a given event is triggered on a target using `actionsForTarget(_:forControlEvent:)`. The method we will use to inform subscribed objects that our control value is updated is `sendActionsForControlEvents(_:)`. You encountered this at the end of the implementation of the setter for the `value` property:

```
self.sendActionsForControlEvents(UIControlEvents.ValueChanged)
```

Calling this method with the `ValueChanged` event is the easiest way to broadcast the information to the entire list of registered targets.

In the example project, a `ThermostatSlider` instance was created in the `viewDidLoad` method of the main view controller (the frame of the slider will be then redefined using auto layout constraints). Here's how:

```
slider = ThermostatSlider(frame: CGRectMake(20, 20, 100, 100))
```

The `updateLabel` selector is then associated with an action for the `ValueChanged` event of the slider, as follows:

```
slider!.addTarget(self,
                  action: "updateLabel",
      forControlEvents: UIControlEvents.ValueChanged)
```

Every time the current value of the slider is updated, the `updateLabel` method will be called, handling the new value as needed. In this example, we just updated a label text by showing the value of the slider.

Customizing the control with UI Appearance

The control that we created in this chapter can be easily customized by modifying its class code directly. A better approach might be leveraging on *UIKit Appearance*, adding more flexibility in the way you (or other developers) can adapt the style of this control without modifying the existent class code. We already discussed this feature in *Chapter 2, UI Components Overview – UIKit*, while discussing `UIKit` controls. Let's take a look at how to use this with your custom control now.

Track colors are the elements that we will customize to obtain a better integration of `ThermostatSlider` with different user interfaces.

The only step to make these properties accessible to UI Appearance is to set them as dynamic, as follows:

```
dynamic var hotTrackColor = UIColor(red:1.0, green:0.4, blue:0.4,
    alpha: 1.0)

dynamic var coldTrackColor = UIColor(red:0.4, green:0.6, blue:1.0,
    alpha: 1.0)
```

Now, from the view controller implementation, you can override the values using the `appearance` proxy and defining the desired colors for all the `ThermostatSlider` instances available in the view; simply execute the following:

```
ThermostatSlider.appearance().hotTrackColor = UIColor.greenColor()

ThermostatSlider.appearance().coldTrackColor = UIColor.redColor()
```

Summary

In this chapter, you saw how to implement a completely custom control by designing an adaptable layout and programming the whole control interaction.

You can experiment a lot with this new topic, and you can also create some new controls that you can (proudly) share with your fellow developers. A really interesting community where you can find inspiration for custom controls is `http://www.cocoacontrols.com`. Users here share their GitHub repositories, and you can try them in real time (with the help of a cool responsive web plugin) or just download the code and play with it!

The next chapter will be a gentle introduction to core graphics, one of the most (in) famous Cocoa frameworks. You will learn the basics of the framework and how to use it to perform even more customized drawing.

Introduction to Core Graphics

9

In the previous chapters, we focused on high-level technologies such as UIKit; then, we moved a step below these to talk about core animation. In this chapter, we will dig even deeper down the system architecture layer and finally reach core graphics, a framework that gives you a multitude of instruments to fully handle 2D drawing on different contexts, such as views, PDF, and bitmap, thanks to the Quartz 2D engine.

All this awesomeness comes at a cost: the effort needed to achieve complex designs is obviously much higher than when you're just using UIKit or core animation. On the bright side, you gain control over powerful tools that grant access to all the freedom you need to create 2D designs programmatically.

Through this chapter, we will talk mainly about these topics:

- The graphic context and graphic state
- UIKitCore graphics helpers
- Drawing with paths

Drawing on the graphic context

Thanks to the core graphics frameworks, you can access the Quartz 2D engine, an API based on interesting drawing tools such as path-based design, color management, transformations, masking, and color blending.

Note that it is common to refer to core graphics and Quartz 2D interchangeably. To be precise, core graphics is the framework that contains Quartz 2D; all the functions of this API use CG as prefix. Quartz 2D is not to be confused with Quartz Core, though. The latter is in fact the framework that contains core animation and core image.

When it comes to using core graphics, the main rule of thumb is that if you want to perform any kind of drawing, you need to get access to a *graphic context*. The context becomes a sort of dashboard where all the drawing operations are executed.

The data type that represents a context is CGContextRef (or just CGContext), which is an opaque object that encapsulates all the information needed to draw, depending on the drawing destination. Here is an overview of the main graphic context types you will work with in iOS:

- **View graphic context**: This is configured when a view is instantiated. You can access this context directly inside the drawRect(_:) method by calling UIGraphicsGetCurrentContext(). As you may note, this method has *UI* as prefix; this is because it is part of the UIKit framework. As you'll learn later, UIKit provides a set of helpers you can use while working with core graphics to simplify some predefined tasks, as in this case, to get the view's graphic context.

- **PDF graphic context**: This allows you to convert your drawings into a PDF document that can contain more than one page. A PDF context can be created with the CGPDFContextCreateWithURL function by specifying the destination of the final file or through CGPDFContextCreate to work directly with the PDF data.

- **Bitmap graphic context**: With this context, you can draw directly into a bitmap image. You can create this context through the UIGraphicsBeginImageContextWithOptions function that receives information, such as the size of the image and the scale factor. You can draw into the context using some of the methods that you will learn about in this chapter; at this point, you need to call UIGraphicsGetImageFromCurrentImageContext to obtain a UIImage representation of your drawing. As a final step, you are responsible for ending the graphic context by calling UIGraphicsEndImageContext.

How drawing works

It is important to look at the context as a painter's canvas, where each drawing action is performed above the previous one, creating a sort of layer hierarchy. If you first draw a square and then create a circle and if the two shapes overlap, you will see the full circle and the portion of square that is not overlapped by the circle. With this logic, you can create complex designs by simply overlapping shapes:

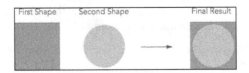

Handling the graphic states

Another analogy with the painter is in the way a brush is defined. Instead of using a brush element, a graphic context uses *graphic states*; in principle, it is really similar to the brush used by the painter, but instead of changing the brush, with a graphic context, you change a property of the brush. Let's say you want to draw a blue rectangle; you define that all the fill color from this point on is going to be blue, then you fill a rectangle, and it will be filled with the blue you defined. Now, if you draw another shape, it will be filled with the same blue color again, because the current graphic state for "fill color" remains blue. There are many other options that you can set in a graphic state — for example, the stroke color, line width, and blend mode.

A really interesting feature of graphic states is the ability to handle a stack of states by calling simple functions. Let's say that you are satisfied with the current blue fill state, but you have a temporary need to draw with other options. You can move the current state on the *stack* by calling the CGContextSaveGState method, update the graphic state with the needed option, and when you are done with the drawing, just get back to the previous state by calling CGContextRestoreGState. This feature is really useful when you have to draw complex elements and want to be sure that the current drawing operation will start from a specific graphic state.

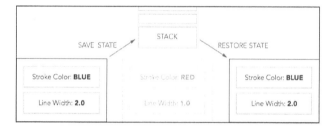

The coordinate system

The coordinate system changes depending on the drawing context. If you get the drawing context from UIView or are drawing in a bitmap context, you will use the same coordinate system UIKit uses, keeping in mind that from Quartz 2D's point of view, it is a *modified coordinate system*. In fact, the *original Quartz 2D coordinate* system is flipped, and it puts the origin (the point where *x* and *y* are equal to 0) at the bottom left of the graphic context:

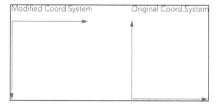

Particular attention needs to be paid when moving the drawing routine from one coordinate system to another, such as when you draw into a PDF graphic context using the same functions that you defined to draw into a view graphic context.

UIKit helpers

Before starting with code, let's have a look at some of the tools provided by UIKit to simplify the drawing process with core graphics. All the functionalities that we will list in this section produce results that can be achieved with core graphics in its "pure" form. You can view these UIKit helpers as shortcuts to some more complex core graphics functions. UIKit and core graphics elements can be easily distinguished by the prefixes of the classes and function names—UI for UIKit and CG for core graphics. You can find all the following code examples in the source code of the chapter.

Drawing with fill and stroke options

The UIKit helpers can be used to alter the current graphic state by defining the current color for *fill* and *stroke* drawing actions. These functionalities are part of the UIColor class with its setFill(), setStroke(), and set() functions (the last sets both the stroke and fill colors). Execute the following code:

```
override func drawRect(rect: CGRect) {
    drawRedRect()
}

func drawRedAndBlackRect(){
    let rect = CGRectMake(10, 10, 30, 30)
    UIColor.redColor().setFill()
    UIColor.blackColor().setStroke()
    UIRectFill(rect)
    UIRectFrame(rect)
}
```

In the preceding code, the drawRedAndBlackRect custom function is called inside the drawRect method. The helper functions can draw directly inside the drawRect method without specifying any context; by default, the *current graphic* context is used. In this specific example, the graphic state for fill and stroke colors is defined through the relative UIColor functions; only then will other helper functions draw a filled rectangle (UIRectFill(rect:)) and a rectangle's stroke above the previous one (UIRectFrame(rect:)). To perform a quick experiment related to the painter model we talked about earlier, let's try to change the drawing sequence. If the stroke function is called before the fill function, only the fill color will be displayed because it completely covers the other rectangle.

Drawing with blending modes

Another option that can be used to define how to draw a rectangle is the blend mode. By setting this information, you can define how an element is drawn in relation to the underlying background. There are many different blend modes accessible through the CGBlendMode enum. Each of these modes defines a mathematical formula that takes into account the color of the shape you are drawing and that of the pixels where the shape will be placed. The result of the formula defines how the two colors will be blended together, producing a single color.

For example, with the *multiply* blend mode, the final color is calculated with this formula:

```
Result = (Top Color) * (Bottom Color) / 255.0
```

Here is an example of two rectangles drawn this way:

```
func drawBlendedRects(){
    let rect_A = CGRectMake(10, 10, 80, 80)
    UIColor.greenColor().setFill()
    UIRectFill(rect_A)

    let rect_B = CGRectMake(30, 30, 80, 80)
    UIColor.redColor().setFill()
    UIRectFillUsingBlendMode(rect_B, CGBlendMode.Multiply)
}
```

The first rectangle is drawn exactly as in the previous example. The fill color is changed before drawing the second rectangle. This rectangle, in turn, is drawn using the UIRectFillUsingBlendMode method with the rectangle frame and the blend mode. The final result is a darker color where the two rectangles overlap:

Drawing with paths

Another really useful set of functionalities was implemented with the UIBezierPath class, a *wrapper* for the core graphics' path drawing functions (which we will talk about in detail later). This class can be adopted to create simple shapes such as rectangles and circles as well as complex shapes that require curved segments.

The most basic example of how to use a Bezier path is the creation of a simple shape. The class provides useful initializers to easily build shaped paths, such as rectangles, rounded rectangles, and ovals. Simply execute the following:

```
func drawBezierRect(){
    let rect = CGRectMake(10, 10, 80, 80)
    let path = UIBezierPath(rect: rect)

    UIColor.blueColor().setStroke()
    path.lineWidth = 5
    path.stroke()
}
```

The `UIBezierPath(rect: rect)` initializer creates a path, then we define the blue stroke color, and we set a thickness for the stroke itself using the `lineWidth` property. Then, the `stroke()` method performs the drawing operation to create the rectangle. The initializer can be replaced with `UIBezierPath(ovalInRect: rect)` to obtain a circle instead.

Under the hood, this helper class creates `CGPath` (this will be discussed in the coming paragraphs) and handles a specific graphic state valid for this path only, where you can define path information (such as the line width). You can access the current `CGPath` through the `cgpath` property, and obviously you can work with it using a mixture of core graphics and `UIBezierPath` functions. We haven't talked about `CGPath` instance yet, but here is a simple example of code that creates a path in core graphics and associates it with `UIBezierPath`, thus showing how they can work together:

```
func cgToBezierRect(){
    let rect = CGRectMake(10, 10, 80, 80)
    let cgPath = CGPathCreateMutable()
    CGPathAddEllipseInRect(cgPath, nil, rect)

let bezierPath = UIBezierPath()
    bezierPath.CGPath = cgPath

UIColor.greenColor().setStroke()
    bezierPath.lineWidth = 5
    bezierPath.stroke()
}
```

The previous code draws a simple circle stroked with a 5-point green line. As you may note, it defines the path through a pure core graphics function, and then it passes the path to an instance of the `UIBezierPath` helper class.

As this is a complete wrapper for `CGPath`, you can also create really complex shapes using quadratic and cubic curves managing curve points. We will talk about these methods later when describing `CGPath`.

The first function that you will encounter while working with core graphics and iOS is probably `UIGraphicsGetCurrentContext`. This allows you to easily get the current context so that you know where to perform any drawing operation. We will use it in the next code example; for now, just keep in mind that it is part of the UIKit framework and not of core graphics.

Drawing with paths

In the previous section, we saw how to simplify drawing paths using `UIBezierPath`. This class is just a wrapper around a set of core graphics functions that allows you to create paths for the current graphic context. In this section, you'll learn how to work with paths using a pure core graphics approach.

As discussed previously, a path is the most basic element that you can use to define a shape. With paths, you can design whichever shape you might have in mind; however, while it is extremely simple to create objects such as lines, squares, and circles, more complex shapes need a little more effort. You will find out soon enough.

Path initialization

A path is, in its essence, a set of one or more shapes (*subpaths*) such as rectangles, complex shapes, or even single lines, arcs, and curves. We already talked about the data type responsible for describing a path: `CGPathRef`, or its mutable version `CGMutablePathRef` (or even just their aliases — `CGPath`/`CGMutablePath`).

You can create a path by calling one of the available initializers for these classes, depending on your needs. If you want to start from a predefined shape, calling one of the predefined shape initializers, such as `CGPathCreateWithRect` or `CGPathCreateWithEllipseInRect`, is the easy way to go. Take a look at the following snippet:

```
func simpleRectPath()->CGPath {
    let rect = CGRect(x: 30, y: 30, width: 80, height: 80)
    let path = CGPathCreateWithRect(rect, nil)

    return path
}
```

You can even initialize an empty mutable path using `CGPathCreateMutable` and add segments and shapes later using CG functions prefixed with *Add* instead of *Create*—for example, `CGPathAddRect`. Run the following code:

```
func simpleMutableRectPath()->CGMutablePath {
    let rect = CGRect(x: 30, y: 30, width: 80, height: 80)
    let path = CGPathCreateMutable()
    CGPathAddRect(path, nil, rect)

    return path
}
```

Building a path

If you need more control, you can use some functions that allow you to build a path using segments. The starting point for the segments is defined by the `CGPathMoveToPoint` function. This receives the current path and the coordinates where the drawing begins. You can then add lines, arcs, or shapes to the path using functions such as `CGPathAddLineToPoint` or `CGPathAddCurveToPoint`. The initial point of the segment created by these functions is the initial point of the path or the end of the previous segment, while the end point is defined as a parameter of the function itself.

In the following example, we will create a path with a single line:

```
func simpleLine()->CGMutablePath{

    let path = CGPathCreateMutable()
    CGPathMoveToPoint(path, nil, 20, 20)
    CGPathAddLineToPoint(path, nil, 100, 100)

    return path
}
```

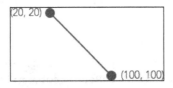

In case you need to create a multisegment path, you can just add more lines (or any other path) and eventually close the path by calling the `CGPathCloseSubpath` function to add a new line that ends at the starting point of the path itself. Here's the code to execute for this:

```
func multiLine()->CGMutablePath{
    let path = CGPathCreateMutable()

    CGPathMoveToPoint(path, nil, 20, 20)

    CGPathAddLineToPoint(path, nil, 100, 100)
    CGPathAddLineToPoint(path, nil, 200, 50)

    CGPathCloseSubpath(path)

    return path
}
```

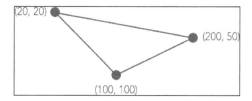

A curve is just a bit more complicated because you need to define the end point and one or two control points, depending on the curve you want to create. The simplest curve is the *quadratic curve*; for this curve, you need to define a single control point, the initial point, and the end points. You can imagine a control point as a force applied to a straight line that changes the line's shape depending on its position and direction. As you may note, the code to create a quadratic curve is remarkably similar to the code needed to create a line:

```
func simpleCurve()->CGMutablePath{

    let path = CGPathCreateMutable()
    CGPathMoveToPoint(path, nil, 20, 20)
    CGPathAddQuadCurveToPoint(path, nil, 100, 20, 100, 100)

    return path
}
```

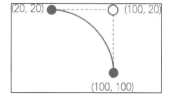

You can obviously mix together different segment types, thus obtaining more complex shapes.

All these functions are prefixed with the *CGPath* word, and as you can see, they don't need a context to create the path. There is another set of similar functions that are prefixed by *CGContext*, though (such as CGContextAddLine and CGContextMoveToPoint). They work in the same exact way. The only difference is that they build the path directly on the context; instead of receiving the path at which to attach the new segments/shapes, they receive the context and build the path directly on it.

Drawing the path

Now that the path is built, it is time to draw it onscreen. As we now know, all drawing operations need a context, so you need to add the path to one before drawing. You don't need this step if you created the path using functions that are prefixed with *CGContext*; otherwise, it is just a matter of calling the CGContextAddPath function, which receives the context and the path to attach it to.

The last step consists in processing the path by calling one of the many functions available to perform the drawing. The most generic is the CGContextDrawPath function that receives the CGPathDrawingMode drawing mode (Stroke, Fill, or FillStroke). Execute the following script:

```
func drawPath(context:CGContext?){
    let rect = CGRect(x: 30, y: 30, width: 80, height: 80)
    let path = CGPathCreateWithRect(rect, nil)

    UIColor.grayColor().setFill()
    UIColor.redColor().setStroke()

    CGContextAddPath(context, path)
    CGContextDrawPath(context, CGPathDrawingMode.FillStroke)
}
```

You can also define the drawing mode directly through the function used to draw the path, such as CGContextStrokePath and CGContextFillPath.

For finer control over the lines, you can update the graphic state by defining options such as line width, line cap/join (the way segments are connected), and color through *CGContext* functions such as CGContextSetLineWidth and CGContextSetLineCap, as follows:

```
CGContextSetLineWidth(context, 2.0)
CGContextSetLineCap(context, CGLineCap.Round)
```

Summary

This chapter was just a brief introduction to such a big topic as core graphics. Nonetheless, it should help you be familiarized with the whole framework pretty easily.

If you're now eager to learn more, gradients, masking, and blending are other extremely helpful components that are worth exploring so that you can get a broader view over this powerful framework.

Index

Thank you for buying
Learning iOS UI Development

About Packt Publishing

Packt, pronounced 'packed', published its first book, *Mastering phpMyAdmin for Effective MySQL Management*, in April 2004, and subsequently continued to specialize in publishing highly focused books on specific technologies and solutions.

Our books and publications share the experiences of your fellow IT professionals in adapting and customizing today's systems, applications, and frameworks. Our solution-based books give you the knowledge and power to customize the software and technologies you're using to get the job done. Packt books are more specific and less general than the IT books you have seen in the past. Our unique business model allows us to bring you more focused information, giving you more of what you need to know, and less of what you don't.

Packt is a modern yet unique publishing company that focuses on producing quality, cutting-edge books for communities of developers, administrators, and newbies alike. For more information, please visit our website at www.packtpub.com.

About Packt Open Source

In 2010, Packt launched two new brands, Packt Open Source and Packt Enterprise, in order to continue its focus on specialization. This book is part of the Packt Open Source brand, home to books published on software built around open source licenses, and offering information to anybody from advanced developers to budding web designers. The Open Source brand also runs Packt's Open Source Royalty Scheme, by which Packt gives a royalty to each open source project about whose software a book is sold.

Writing for Packt

We welcome all inquiries from people who are interested in authoring. Book proposals should be sent to author@packtpub.com. If your book idea is still at an early stage and you would like to discuss it first before writing a formal book proposal, then please contact us; one of our commissioning editors will get in touch with you.

We're not just looking for published authors; if you have strong technical skills but no writing experience, our experienced editors can help you develop a writing career, or simply get some additional reward for your expertise.

Unity3D UI Essentials

ISBN: 978-1-78355-361-7   Paperback: 280 pages

Leverage the power of the new and improved UI system for Unity to enhance your games and apps

1. Discover how to build efficient UI layouts coping with multiple resolutions and screen sizes.

2. In-depth overview of all the new UI features that give you creative freedom to drive your game development to new heights.

3. Walk through many different examples of UI layout from simple 2D overlays to in-game 3D implementations.

Learning iOS Security

ISBN: 978-1-78355-174-3   Paperback: 142 pages

Enhance the security of your iOS platform and applications using iOS-centric security techniques

1. Familiarize yourself with fundamental methods to leverage the security of iOS platforms and apps.

2. Resolve common vulnerabilities and security-related shortcomings in iOS applications and operating systems.

3. A pragmatic and hands-on guide filled with clear and simple instructions to develop a secure mobile deployment.

Please check **www.PacktPub.com** for information on our titles

Learning iOS Forensics

ISBN: 978-1-78355-351-8   Paperback: 220 pages

A practical hands-on guide to acquire and analyze iOS devices with the latest forensic techniques and tools

1. Perform logical, physical, and file system acquisition along with jailbreaking the device.

2. Get acquainted with various case studies on different forensic toolkits that can be used.

3. A step-by-step approach with plenty of examples to get you familiarized with digital forensics in iOS.

Learning iOS 8 Game Development Using Swift

ISBN: 978-1-78439-355-7   Paperback: 366 pages

Create robust and spectacular 2D and 3D games from scratch using Swift – Apple's latest and easy-to-learn programming language

1. Create engaging games from the ground up using SpriteKit and SceneKit.

2. Boost your game's visual performance using Metal - Apple's new graphics library.

3. A step-by-step approach to exploring the world of game development using Swift.

Please check **www.PacktPub.com** for information on our titles